D1099203

091171

What can I do with … an arts degree?
This first edition published in 2002 by Trotman and Company Ltd
2 The Green, Richmond, Surrey TW9 1PL

© Trotman and Company Limited 2002

Statistics from *What do Graduates do?* are quoted with kind
permission from AGCAS.

The HESA data quoted in this publication is from the HESA Student
Record July 2000; © Higher Education Statistics Agency Limited
2001.

The Higher Education Statistics Agency (HESA) does not accept any
responsibility for any inferences or conclusions derived from the
data quoted in this publication by third parties.

British Library Cataloguing in Publication Data
A catalogue record for this book is available from the British Library

ISBN 0 85660 722 3

Typeset by Mac Style Ltd, Scarborough, N. Yorkshire

Printed and bound in Great Britain by Creative Print and Design
(Wales) Ltd

Contents

About the author

Beryl Dixon is an experienced careers adviser who has worked in different careers companies and in a tertiary college where she advised students of all ages on employment and higher education choices. She has also worked for the Ministry of Defence and the Department for Education and Skills, visiting schools in Hong Kong, Cyprus, Brussels and Luxembourg to provide careers advice to the children of expatriate service personnel and government officials.

She now concentrates on careers writing and is the author of several books on careers and higher education. She also writes for a number of careers publications, including *Youcan*, UCAS's magazine for A-level students and for national newspapers including *The Times* and the *Independent*. Her other titles published by Trotman are *Getting into Art and Design*, *Getting into Hospitality*, *Getting into Languages* and *How to Choose your Postgraduate Course*.

She is herself a modern languages graduate.

Acknowledgements

I would like to thank Clare Wright of Birmingham University Careers Advisory Service, Jeff Goodman of Bristol University Careers Advisory Service, Kevin Thompson of Reading University Careers Advisory Service, Claire Rees of York University Careers Advisory Service and Carl Gilleard, Chief Executive of the Association of Graduate Recruiters, for their assistance when I was researching this book.

Introduction

Forty per cent of the 18-plus age group now go through higher education. The government's aim is 50% but there are signs that there is some resistance among the 10% in question. Nevertheless the increase in the number of courses on offer has been spectacular. There are now over 5000 different course titles listed in the UCAS handbook – offered by 332 higher education institutions (universities and colleges). The year 2003 will see one more. A completely new university is to be built in Falmouth to serve would-be students in Cornwall, most of whom currently have to leave the county for their higher education.

What are the benefits of higher education? Why should so many young people flock to do degrees? And thereby make a major investment?

The most obvious benefit is financial. The median starting salary for a graduate in 2001 was approximately £19,000, with some lucky recruits being paid in excess of £36,000! Don't forget though that that is the median. If some people are earning £36,000 then others are earning £11,000. The lowest starting salary reported in a survey conducted by the Institute of Employment Studies for the Association of Graduate Recruiters (AGR) was £10,900.* The highest starting salaries were offered by legal and financial firms.

Starting salaries for graduates had increased by 5.5% on the previous year and AGR expects them to rise again, by 4.1%, for 2002.

---

* *2001 Graduate Salaries and Vacancies*, AGR, July 2001.

1

All surveys show that most people who went through higher education earn more then those who did not. According to a survey, *Rewards for Learning* by the Institute of Fiscal Studies in 1996, the hourly pay for men aged 33 with a first degree was 21% higher than for those with A-levels; for women it was 39%. And, in corroboration of the 1996 survey, research conducted at the London School of Economics in 2001 found that male graduates increased their earnings by 30% over those with A-levels; female graduates by 29%.

Do graduates automatically find more interesting jobs than non-graduates? With an ever-increasing number of students going on to higher education there is more competition for graduate jobs. And what exactly is a graduate job? Certainly some graduates are doing jobs nowadays that would once have been done by 18-year-old entrants. Some complain that their ability is under-utilised. On the other hand many employers want more highly educated people who can introduce change and make things happen. It is never a good idea to look at data relating to first jobs only to see what graduates typically end up doing. Quite often it is necessary to gain experience in a lower-level job before being fully stretched. Research by the University of Warwick shows that fewer than 10% of graduates are still in 'non-graduate' jobs three and a half years after graduation and at that point only 2% of economically active graduates (those available for work) were unemployed.

Is it true that it is only those students who have done vocational degrees and acquired technical skills who get well-paid jobs? The purpose of this book is to show that this is not so. Students are often dissuaded from doing an arts (or humanities) subject because it is not seen as leading to any particular careers.

The main benefit of higher education is that graduates should gain some key transferable skills that are valued by employers. 'Should' because although some skills come with the degree-level study others are gained through different aspects of university or college life. A constant theme throughout this book will be the need to acquire such skills. **A degree alone is no guarantee of a job**. Employers look for certain kinds of people. Between 35% and 40% of jobs advertised for graduates do not specify a degree subject. More important then than your in-depth knowledge of ancient Rome or Milton's sonnets are your general level of ability and your transferable skills (ie those that can be used in any job). A student with a First in history who has spent three years sitting in the library to achieve it is not sought after by too many employers. A student with a 2:1 who has taken part in a range of extra-curricular activities and had a part-time job is a much more likely prospect.

This book looks at the skills and qualifications most required by employers and the activities that students can use to 'add value' to their CVs. It includes advice from both employers and careers advisers. There are also individual chapters on Classics, English, History, History of Art, Modern Languages and Philosophy, showing any general trends in employment from students of those subjects. However, please do not think that certain careers automatically follow certain subjects. What can be done by a historian should be equally possible for a modern linguist or classics graduate.

The subjects were chosen by virtue of their being strictly non-vocational. They could equally well have been social sciences such as politics or sociology. We could have included geography. We could have made the title more general and asked, 'What can I do with my degree?', since the object of the book is to point out the value of higher education and of the transferable skills that graduates gain. Examples of biologists in sales or engineers in merchant banking could then have been included to stress the fact that it is never necessary to use a degree subject directly in a career, even if it appears to be career directed. Modern languages are included because as every careers adviser knows, contrary to students' perceptions, languages alone are rarely sufficient. They are an *asset* in many careers rather than a vocational qualification in themselves. This theme is developed in Chapter 7.

But it is prospective arts graduates who most frequently ask 'What could I do with philosophy?' or 'Where would history lead me other than into teaching?' So, if you are planning to take an arts degree or are already on an arts course at university or college, this book is for you.

A large part of the book consists of case studies of recent graduates describing their careers since graduating and listing the skills that they feel their degree courses equipped them with or developed. When researching the book I contacted a number of universities and colleges of higher education asking if it was possible to put me in touch with graduates from six subjects who were using their degrees in different ways. You can read about the experiences of some of them in Chapters 3–8. The response from some institutions was so enthusiastic that kind offers had to be declined either for reasons of space or because the particular jobs had already been included. The case studies were chosen to represent a good cross section, and I had to leave out:

★ classics graduates working as a picture librarian, a retail manager and a public relations executive
★ one philosophy graduate working as a freelance computer programmer and writing a novel in his spare time; another in international news editing in broadcasting
★ several art historians in publishing
★ languages graduates in investment banking, accountancy and market research
★ an English graduate in air traffic control; another in media planning and buying
★ one history graduate working as a solicitor and one as a VAT officer.

One university kindly allowed me to search its database showing the whereabouts of previous students, but when I contacted some for various reasons they did not wish to be featured. However, just to give a flavour of yet more openings for arts graduates, they were working as:

★ a production controller for a frozen foods manufacturer (English and French);
★ a charity fundraiser (French and art history);
★ an NHS manager (English);
★ a trainee solicitor (History);
★ an insurance broker (German);
★ VAT visiting officers (History; English with art);
★ in insurance sales manager (English);
★ an assistant project officer with a county council's conservation unit (Philosophy);
★ an administrator with the Open University (Modern languages).

1   Myths and facts

So just what can you do with an arts degree? You cannot, obviously, become an engineer, architect, doctor, pharmacist, rocket scientist – or a host of other things for which a vocational degree and professional training are prerequisites. But that still leaves a lot! Not so sure? Then how about:

Accountant:
Certified
Chartered
Management
Public Finance
Administrator
Advertising:
Account Executive
Copywriter
Air Traffic
   Controller
Antique Dealer
Archivist
Army Officer
Arts
   Administrator
Auctioneer and
   Valuer
Bank Manager
Barrister
Bookseller
Broadcasting:
Editor
Producer
Programme Assistant
Reporter

Building Society
   Manager
Buyer
Careers Adviser
Charity
   Fundraiser
Civil Servant
Company
   Secretary
Computer
   Programmer
Conference
   and/or Events
   Manager
Customs and
   Excise Officer
Diplomat
Estate or
   Lettings Agent
Financial
   Adviser
Freight
   Forwarder
Health Service
   Manager
Hotel Manager

Housing
   Manager
Human
   Resources
   (Personnel)
   Officer
Immigration
   Officer
Indexer
Information
   Manager/
   Scientist
IT Consultant
Insurance:
Broker
Claims Assessor
Underwriter
Journalist
Leisure Manager
Librarian
Local
   Government
   Officer
Logistics
   Manager
Loss Adjuster

Management
Consultant
Marketing
Manager
Market Research
Executive
Merchant Navy
Officer
Museum Curator
Naval Officer
Police Officer
Prison Governor
Probation
Officer
Public Relations
Executive

Publishing:
Editor
Picture Researcher
Proof Reader
Purchasing
Officer
RAF Officer
Recruitment
Consultant
Retail
Manager
Royal Marines
Officer
Social Worker
Solicitor
Surveyor

Tourism
Manager
Tourist
Information
Centre
Manager
Training Officer/
Manager
Travel Industry
Manager
Youth and
Community
Worker
Web Designer.

For the following careers a postgraduate qualification is essential – irrespective of first-degree subject:

Barrister
Librarian
Probation Officer
Social Worker
Solicitor
Surveyor
Teacher (in a state school).

You do not always have to do a full-time course (and find the necessary funding). *Some* relevant courses may be done on a part-time basis while you work in an unrelated job to keep body and soul together. (If any of the careers that require further qualifications interest you, you can find all the information you need on entry and training routes in a good careers reference book. For suggested titles see Chapter 10.)

In the following careers, completion of a postgraduate course may help to gain entry where there is competition for jobs.

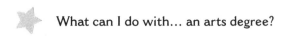

Again, part-time courses are available.

    Archivist
    Arts Administrator
    Auctioneer and Valuer
    Careers Adviser
    Computer Programmer
    Financial Adviser
    Hotel Manager
    Human Resources (Personnel) Officer
    Information Manager/Information Scientist
    Journalist
    Leisure Manager
    Logistics Manager
    Museum Curator
    Public Relations Executive
    Tourism Manager
    Tourist Information Centre Manager
    Travel Industry Manager.

All graduates should be aware of the fact that study does not always end with a degree! Many of the careers listed above – and even some careers entered by students who have taken vocational degrees – require further study for professional examinations. Would-be accountants, for example, join their employers as trainees (confusingly known as *students* if they are in chartered accountancy). They are trained by their employers, learn while doing the job but have to work in their spare time towards professional examinations set by the different accountancy bodies. Only when they pass these exams do they become fully qualified. Air traffic controllers, company secretaries, probation officers, social workers and financial advisers – including stockbrokers – *must* obtain appropriate qualifications in order to practise their professions. In other careers qualifications exist but are optional. Having said that, many employers will expect graduates to obtain them. You would be unlikely to progress very far without taking the examinations of the Chartered Institute of Bankers or of the Chartered Insurance Institute. Most newspaper editors will expect trainee journalists to obtain the National Council for the Training of Journalists' qualifications and most organisations would want their human resources staff to become qualified through the Chartered Institute of Personnel and Development – and so on.

Several of the graduates who feature as case studies in this book refer to their examinations and to the amount of time taken up in studying for them.

Myth

★ Arts graduates become teachers.
★ Arts graduates are unemployable.
★ Arts graduates are limited to a very narrow range of careers according to the subject they studied. (English graduates all go into publishing or journalism; historians into archive or museum work.)

Fact

★ Between 35% and 40% of jobs advertised for graduates do not require a specific degree subject.
★ Arts graduates have a general level of ability and certain skills valued by employers. (However, for some careers, a postgraduate diploma or degree is either necessary or smooths the way.)
★ Many people doing the same jobs have degrees in English, history, music or even chemistry or engineering.
★ Further study is often required to gain professional qualifications.

2 The rounded individual or what employers want

Why do companies employ graduates? As mentioned earlier, as far as arts graduates are concerned it is rarely for your specific subject knowledge. Rather it is because studying an academic subject at degree level has given you certain intellectual skills plus a level of personal maturity. Arts graduates can:

★ **Reason.** Arts courses place great emphasis on essay writing, seminar and tutorial work. They teach students to form their own opinions. Often, students have to reach a compromise *or* present the best possible case given the circumstances and the evidence available. There is no 'set in stone' correct answer.

★ **Analyse.** Before they can present their case they have to assess and evaluate information – huge amounts of it – in order to write certain essays or seminar papers. They learn to deal with vast amounts of material and select what is relevant.

★ **They have trained minds.**

★ **They can also communicate**. On most arts courses students give presentations. Students lead discussion groups, giving their analysis of a text, topic or situation, and respond to comments from staff and other students. They have to defend their views under pressure. *Hopefully* they also learn to respond to criticism positively, listen to other people and accept their points of view. (Listening is an important part of communication.)

★ In addition they are able to **take responsibility for their own learning and to manage their time**. Seven or eight hours of lectures each week leave a lot of free time, with all kinds of temptations to use it unwisely. It may be difficult at first – but eventually most students learn the arts of self-discipline and time management.

These skills however are not enough to guarantee an interesting job, or indeed any job at all. They must be allied to what most recruiters call personal, transferable skills. They are also known as *core* or *key* skills.

New patterns of work have emerged. The traditional structure contains jobs in which as a manager you would be in charge of a team of people and be responsible for their work. In turn you would report to someone more senior – your own manager. In time you would hope for promotion and a range of increasingly senior jobs. Managers do not merely supervise and carry out instructions however. They are expected to think, come up with ideas and contribute to their organisation's development.

But in many organisations, particularly in the consultancy, IT, financial and communications industries, teams are formed to work on individual projects. Each member contributes his or her area of expertise to the project. When it ends, the members leave to begin work on different projects. In this type of employment you might work with some of the same people again; with others never. You might be the team leader (in effect, the manager) on one project and a team member on the next. The ability to form working relationships quickly is crucial in this kind of employment. The skill of senior managers is in assigning the right combination of people to a project.

In both structures of employment the ability to relate well to other people is important. Both Nicholas Chalmers, a hotel manager (see page 56) and Jeremy Silverman, a management consultant, (page 75) refer to this. Jeremy works in different teams, which may even change during the course of a project; Nicholas needs to be able to explain to people why decisions have been made and why he wants things done in a certain way.

So it is hardly surprising that one of the top skills sought by graduate employers – recruiting to both structures – is communication. This is closely followed by several other skills that are common to nearly all employers, regardless of their line of business. So common are they that two or three years ago when Marks & Spencer realised they had over-recruited, and had to inform a number of prospective graduate management trainees that their jobs were no longer available, they received requests from other employers – not only other retailers but ones as different as accountants and IT consultants – to be put in touch with the students. These employers reasoned that if the students had already been selected by one major organisation they would be equally suited to working for them.

The top ten skills are (not in descending order):

★ adaptability
★ commercial awareness
★ communication, both oral and written
★ initiative
★ leadership
★ numeracy
★ persuasive powers
★ problem-solving ability
★ self-reliance
★ teamwork.

Some people add willingness to learn, commitment, ability to cope under pressure, desire to achieve, reliability, but most of these fit into the ten general headings.

What do they mean in the employment context?

Adaptability

No job stays the same for long. In two years' time you could be doing very different work. You might have to retrain. Almost certainly you will have to attend short courses or make sure in other ways that you constantly update the skills you need to do the current job. You might need to acquire new ones to deal with the way in which it is changing.

Commercial awareness

If private sector businesses don't make profits they fail; public sector organisations have tight budgets to meet. Employers are always looking to increase their income and decrease their costs. Graduates need to understand the implications of this and understand why the apparently perfect solution just won't do. In many jobs they also need to understand the importance of the customer/client/patient – who of course is always right!

Communication

At work you must not only communicate with colleagues but possibly with customers and suppliers. You might soon have to supervise or manage junior staff. You will almost certainly have to produce written reports. You might have to explain things to people who do not share your level of knowledge.

Then there will be meetings. Many people find these difficult at first. Everyone is present to discuss an issue. They want to fight their own corner. But time is limited. The chairman or woman may not allocate enough. Your arguments must be rehearsed, ready, foolproof – but ready to be adapted and restated if necessary. Time to think on your feet! The meeting might even be badly chaired, with some people allowed to be too dominant. Time for diplomacy.

Initiative

In most graduate jobs employers don't want people who simply do as they are told and keep the current system running smoothly. They want innovators with ideas, who will challenge the status quo and improve on it. (See also **Self-reliance** below.)

Leadership

This is not simply implementing a strategy by telling people what to do. They may need to be convinced, persuaded, helped to do what you expect of them.

Numeracy

Unfortunately for you, if you dropped maths with a great sigh of relief after GCSE, most jobs involve some numbers. There is a big difference though between understanding and feeling comfortable with figures, graphs and charts (numeracy) and the finer aspects of calculus, geometry and algebra (maths).

Persuasive powers

Back to the meetings! Or to all sorts of problems both with colleagues and with potential clients, suppliers and so on. Being able to get your own way (if you are right!) through negotiation and diplomacy is a very valuable skill.

Problem-solving ability

Fairly self-evident. But at work you won't just have academic arguments to weigh up. There will be constraints due to budget problems, timescale or lack of employees with the right skills. Your beautiful solution may need a lot of adaptation and compromise. You may well need to work under pressure. *You will have already coped with this in exam conditions.*

Self-reliance

After some initial or induction training you will be expected to stand on your own feet and not need constant supervision. This does not mean floundering, afraid to ask for help. The skill in managing your own learning is in knowing to what point you can carry on and at what point you need to ask for clarification or assistance.

The way in which graduates are trained is changing. Once companies took a small number of high fliers, seen as having potential for senior management, and put them through carefully structured training programmes of up to two years. During this time the graduates gained experience in most departments in the company. Some companies still recruit fairly small numbers (in relation to the increased number of graduates now available) on to this type of scheme. But many employers now recruit graduates directly into specific jobs – and expect them to begin to contribute almost immediately. Even where the traditional programme exists trainees are not supernumerary trainees. Throughout the training period they are given real work to do while they are gaining their experience. There is consequently a need for graduates who can use their initiative and take charge of their own learning.

Teamwork

This means working with and for other people and getting the best out of the situation.

Some employers' viewpoints

Carl Gilleard is the Chief Executive of the Association of Graduate Recruiters (AGR), an organisation representing over 600 companies that employ graduates. He says,

'We regularly ask our members which skills they require from graduate entrants. Consistently at the top are interpersonal skills and teamwork. The others are:

★ problem-solving ability
★ communication
★ time management
★ computer literacy
★ numeracy
★ flexibility.

'Moving up the list are:

★ cultural sensitivity
★ customer orientation or awareness
★ business awareness.

'Employees need to be sensitive these days to other people's backgrounds and sensitivities – in all companies, but particularly in those operating in the global marketplace. Willingness to take risks, entrepreneurial skill and innovation are also frequently mentioned.'

Mr Gilleard finds from his own experience as an employer that both flexibility and interpersonal skills are particularly important, especially in the small and medium-sized enterprises where many graduates are now employed.

'We have a small staff here and everyone turns their hand to any task that needs to be done. For the first 30 minutes here today I was the Chief Executive. For the next hour I unloaded the boxes containing new computer equipment for the office that I had been to buy personally yesterday – and set it up. We give high priority to customer service here. Employers, the media and students are all our customers. We do not leave the phone ringing. Whoever is nearest when it goes, including myself, answers. We do not keep our customers waiting. Graduates need to appreciate that in small firms they have to be prepared to work at different levels.

'As for interpersonal skills – in a previous job I had one member of staff who was intellectually brilliant but could not work with other people. When I discussed this with him his response was that he would really have been happier in a backroom job. I challenge anyone to think of an example of such a thing. Every job requires you to communicate with colleagues if not with outsiders.'

Advice from Mr Gilleard

'Recognise your skills. Don't be dismissive. I have all too often heard students say "I have only ever worked in a bar or a fast food outlet ..." What skills they could extract from that! I have queued for burgers with my children and seen how they work under pressure, keep their tempers when customers change their orders, work at speed, keep up the pace – and smile.

'Show enthusiasm when it comes to jobhunting. Research the company and look interested. Who does a recruiter remember at the end of a long day behind a stand at a recruitment fair?! They want bright, lively people who will inspire others.'

Accenture

Accenture (formerly Andersen Consulting) advises some of the world's biggest companies and recruits a large number of graduates globally. It normally recruits 500 a year in the UK alone. It looks for graduates 'who have commanding intellectual skills as well as the ability to work well with people'. Graduate Recruitment Manager, Ben Johnston, himself a classicist, says,

'We do not set out to look for any particular degree subject. On average, about 40% of our intake come from arts and social science backgrounds, many from classics, music and philosophy. Interestingly, we have tried to see if there is any correlation between subject studied and success in our company. There is none. Our most senior staff have a variety of backgrounds.'

Recruits from science and humanities subjects have different skills, says Mr Johnston. Which ones are common to arts graduates?

'They are able to work on their own initiative as they have been largely left to their own devices for a major part of the time. Some have had as few as six or seven hours of lectures. The responsibility for preparing essays and completing their work on time has been theirs. They have organisational and planning skills and can carry out their own research. They have the ability to differentiate between several conclusions. Whereas a mathematician or engineer may endeavour to come up with the right answer, an arts graduate is used to assessing different arguments and presenting the benefits of each. In working life it is rare to have the perfect solution. There are shades of ambiguity. Every decision reached has to be the best one possible given the circumstances. Finally, giving oral presentations is a usual feature of most arts courses.

'The ability to communicate via e-mail is important. That is a difficult medium. People leave short e-mails these days instead of long phone messages. The wording has to be just right – it can easily be misinterpreted.

'However, we do look for a common set of skills in *all* our trainees. Under five main headings these are:

★ **Impact** – demonstrated by coming through as a confident communicator at interview. Our staff are constantly meeting new people and relating to new clients. They will be working with people from very different backgrounds. One week they could be doing a consultancy project in an investment bank; the next in a local authority office. Clients might be in their 40s while they are still in their 20s.
★ **Leadership ability**. How well will they deal as a leader with other people? We are looking for management potential in all new entrants.
★ **Ability to work in a team** – not necessarily with the same people for long. We form new teams to work on different projects – taking into account individuals' expertise.
★ **The ability to analyse problems** – ie intellectual ability.
★ **Interest in and understanding of what Accenture does.**'

The National Health Service

The NHS runs two national training schemes annually: one for general management, the other for financial management. They are open to both recent graduates and to career changers. Marita Brown, the National Scheme Manager, recruits 60 trainees for each scheme annually. Why does the NHS need graduates? Ms Brown replies,

'Because a degree demonstrates a certain level of attainment. Graduates are also likely to have had the chance to develop the skills we require and those with one or two years' post-degree work experience have an added maturity. In fact we find that very few new graduates apply to us. They are likely to have worked in non-professional jobs for a while or travelled before deciding to settle into a professional career. That too brings added maturity.

'However, the degree alone is not enough – and that is why the subject is irrelevant. We take trainees from a wide variety of degree courses. What is important is that they have the skills we assess against. These are:

★ **Communication.** NHS managers deal with people from all kinds of backgrounds, hospital employees, senior clinicians and patients. Many now work outside hospital settings, delivering primary care. In the community they work with GPs, nurses, pharmacists, opticians and patient groups. All must be consulted about proposed changes. One woman left the scheme and was immediately placed in a hospital where she was in charge of six members of staff, all in their 40s and 50s. They had worked there for years and were set in their ways of work. She needed the communication skills to win them over and persuade them to take her seriously. She had to show that although she was young she had just completed a course of training that equipped her to manage.

★ **Ability to influence and negotiate.** Managers work with very disparate groups both in hospitals and in primary health care teams. Consultants, other clinical staff and managers of various departments within a hospital or NHS Trust all hold their own views on the ways in which things should be run. In the community GPs are independent contractors – and also have their own views. Linked with this skill is that of ability to **respect diversity** – to understand other people's cultures and attitudes.

★ **Ability to implement change.** Applicants would need to demonstrate to us that they had been in a situation where this had taken place – either in their academic, social or home life. Had they for example changed the way in which a student society was run or made improvements to it? Our scheme places strong emphasis on the need to modernise the NHS.

★ **Leadership and teamwork.** We would look for examples on the application form or at interview of instances where they had to work with other people, including difficult ones – and how they resolved any problems.'

And where are graduates lacking?

> 'They often lack the ability to consider wider issues. They may have focused entirely on their own narrow world. The NHS is a hugely complex organisation. I could use the example of a student society again. Have they ever thought "What are we trying to achieve in our own society and how does that fit in with the aims of other ones?" Or "Are we helping the student community as a whole?" Work experience, in whatever kind of job, can help to develop this skill.'

Procter & Gamble

Procter & Gamble sells over 300 products, including well-known brand name cosmetics, household products and foods, in 150 countries. It recruits graduates into a range of careers. Specific subject degrees are required for entry to research, development and product supply, but the following jobs are open to graduates in any discipline – including, obviously, arts subjects: customer business development, financial management, human resources, IT and marketing.

Why does the company recruit graduates? For their general level of intellect, says Recruitment and Diversity Manager Charlotte Griffiths – plus a range of personal skills. Applicants are expected to give examples of these in their CVs. Ms Griffiths defines these skills as follows:

★ **Leadership** – the ability to set clear directions for people, to motivate them and keep them on track. Examples of leadership ability could include having run a society, raised funds for a project (and shown tenacity in hanging on when things have started to go wrong).
★ **Capacity** – the ability to improve one's own learning and development, to train others and to streamline processes in order to make them more efficient. Successful candidates will have pursued a range of interests but be able to demonstrate strong commitment to at least one (showing the ability to take something on and see it through).

★ **Risk taking**. Companies need people who will take informed (not reckless) risks, people who will evaluate a situation and be prepared to move forward when 100% of the facts are not known. (A company that hesitates too long, perhaps waiting to hold just one more consumer test on a new product, can find itself beaten to the marketplace by a rival.) The risk takers should also be capable of analysing what went wrong if necessary and evaluating their actions to see whether failure could have been avoided.

Ms Griffiths says,

'It means being assertive in uncertainty, and is the most difficult skill to explain. But it could be demonstrated by someone who is the first person from their family to go through higher education, who has stepped into the unknown; or by someone who has travelled and stood on their own two feet. We had one applicant who impressed because at a university whose student union was proposing to ban the armed services from recruiting on campus, because of their anti-gay policy, he stood up at a meeting and argued for them to be allowed the visit. He was not gay himself but felt strongly that the ban would also be discriminatory. He took a risk in standing up for his beliefs.'

★ **Innovation** – an entrepreneurial streak. Someone with this skill can apply creativity to obtain a result, can think in new ways and, by combining logic with some unconventional thinking, can apply variations on ideas developed in one situation to another.
★ **Solutions** – ie problem-solving ability.
★ **Collaboration** – a combination of the ability to work with other people – ie teamwork – and communication. Procter & Gamble is a global company. Project teams are formed from staff working all over the world. Team members need to be sensitive to other cultures and other people's backgrounds. They must be able to express their own opinions while respecting the views of others.

Selection procedures

These begin with an application form. The more well known the organisation the more demanding their forms! Don't expect to get away with simply giving some personal details. Today's forms usually include tricky questions along the lines of, 'Describe a major achievement that you are proud of'; 'Use this space to describe a problem or difficulty you have overcome and how'; or 'Give examples of occasions when you have used leadership skills'. Difficult? Well, perhaps not exactly easy – but how do arts students spend a large proportion of their time if not in thinking, assessing, making notes and then presenting a case?

Many large companies have a selection process that consists of several stages. First, company representatives visit universities on what is known as the *milk round*. (Smaller nowadays than it used to be but still used by large recruiters, the milk round got its name because it is there to cream off the best talent.) Students have initial interviews during which their application forms are discussed and they are asked a number of basic questions regarding their interests and motivation for applying to the company. Those who pass the initial stage are invited to an assessment day (or days). This is where the fun starts. Patterns obviously vary from company to company but usually consist of some or all of the following:

★ written tests of verbal reasoning, numeracy and often personality;
★ group discussions;
★ individual presentations;
★ one-to-one interviews – much more detailed now than the initial ones.

You might be asked to give a prepared presentation lasting a certain length of time. Or one prepared on the spot. Lisa Kelly (see page 67) was asked to think on her feet and speak instantly on a topic she had just been given and convince the rest of the group that her arguments were correct. In small groups you might be asked to discuss a topic unrelated to your job application (and therefore requiring no preparation) *or* an aspect of the work of the company. Recruiters observe and assess how well candidates are performing against a checklist of skills they are looking for. **Your training as an arts graduate will stand you in good stead for this type of selection procedure.**

The non-academic skills and you

Question: How can you acquire any missing skills?
Answer: Through extra-curricular activities. Higher education is not simply about getting a degree. It is about developing as a person. All those readily available and relatively cheap sports and leisure activities have a dual purpose. They are not just fun. They can positively add to your CV.

Do take any opportunity you can to develop a wide range of interests. This will prove to potential employers that you can manage your time. (Here you are with a good class of degree and yet you also spent hours a week on the sports field, in the orchestra, not to mention the union bar. And you probably held down a part-time job as well. So, not someone who is going to crack when asked to handle several problems at the same time or meet a tight deadline.)

Better still, make one of your interests a major one – and take an active part in organising. Avoid a list of activities in which you always had things done for you and were the passenger.

Adaptability

Any evidence that you like new environments, travel or have worked or lived in different places will be an advantage. Modern linguists who have spent a period abroad or students in other subjects who have done so through the ERASMUS programme or in a gap year often refer to the personal benefits both of standing on their own feet and of sampling other cultures.

Commercial awareness

Even that tedious job that you do to keep body and soul together comes in useful here. Take note of everything that you see at work and draw from it. You might see examples of poor service. You might have the chance to improve them. When you are asked at a job interview what you know about commerce you can draw on the list.

Communication

Don't hang back in seminars. Take every opportunity to give presentations. You might be nervous at first but so will most other students (despite appearances!). You could also get a job in a shop, bar or telephone call centre – all luckily now typical student jobs – where talking to people is essential.

Initiative

Can you make things happen? Have you organised an event? Raised funds? Been responsible for implementing any change – getting hall of residence menus changed or negotiating a change to the course syllabus, through membership of relevant committees? Have you started a club?

Leadership

You might much rather be one of the group, but don't be afraid to take the lead when you get the opportunity. Employers want people who could become managers.

Numeracy

Don't let your mental arithmetic get rusty. You might have to pass a numerical aptitude test as part of a company's selection process. If you can get a job in a busy bar taking drinks orders that should not be a problem. You could also enquire whether your careers service offers the possibility of sitting a practice numeracy test – and do some revision or arrange some coaching if you have difficulty with it.

Persuasive powers

Can you coax your flatmates into doing their fair share of the shopping and housework? Can you keep your cool in shops or restaurants when you are not happy with something? Could you strike a good deal if you were selling something? If you are not sure, watch people who are good at this and learn from them.

Problem-solving ability

Problem solving does not occur only in academic work. There must be instances in part-time jobs or in any extra-curricular activities where this ability is useful. It is a good idea to keep a list or log of such instances in case that dreaded question, 'Describe how you have overcome a difficult situation' comes up on an application form.

Self-reliance

Most students live away from home and learn to cope. What about adding some independent travel in the vacations? Not a package holiday but a journey that you plan yourself.

Teamwork

Employers prefer people who participate in activities rather than spend all their time in the library or are interested in sport only as spectators. Build up evidence of membership of sports teams, committees, voluntary work projects, societies, choirs, a group that went on a field trip … Possibilities are endless.

Where arts graduates may fall down is in the areas of *numeracy* and *commercial awareness.* But there is one more weapon you can add to your armoury. You can gain some commercial awareness, possibly improve your numerical skills – and develop many of the other skills – by undertaking a period of work experience. Don't get to the end of a degree course without it!

There are some really good schemes, such as the Shell STEP Programme. You could ask your careers service about this and about companies that provide *internships* (paid vacation work experience). Jeremy Silverman (page 75) did one during his languages course, as did Tom Broadhurst, who did classics (page 32). This option is, of course, open to all students – not just those doing arts subjects. The economics of student life mean that you probably have a part-time job. You can learn a lot, from even the most boring work, that could be used to impress at an eventual interview (working with people from different backgrounds, customer service, IT, observing how a business is run etc).

Classics 3

Classics is far from being a useless subject. Indeed classics students go into an extremely wide range of careers. The subject equips students to be versatile – probably because, as one of the graduates who features as a case study points out, it covers a variety of disciplines.

So what do you gain from studying classics?

You will develop logical thought processes. Both Latin and Greek are extremely logical. (Not surprisingly, many classicists become computer programmers or head for some kind of analytical work.) The two languages require care and attention to detail – all those case endings and grammatical agreements. In addition you will acquire many of the skills also gained by people who have studied literature or history, depending on the slant of the course and the options you choose. These include communication skills, both oral and written. You will doubtless have to present papers or read reports to a group. You will, in common with all arts students, be expected to research and produce essays. You will study different societies and cultures that will encourage flexibility in thinking and you will need to be very disciplined, since you are unlikely to have many lectures each week. In a sense you will get the best of both worlds – the ability to discuss and reason on topics for which there is no definitive answer plus the ability to provide very precise answers to certain questions where there is a right answer – in translation work. Your direct subject knowledge, however, is likely to be of little relevance in a future career unless you decide to teach, get a job as an editor with a publisher of classical textbooks – or like one graduate (not included in this book) – are able to think on your feet and impress an interviewer with your knowledge of retailing derived from studying ancient marketplaces!

The most obvious careers for classicists then are teaching and publishing. The subject also leads students to careers in archive work and museum curatorship. Classics is useful in any career requiring analytical ability, such as law, the Civil Service, computing and IT, and certain careers in finance such as insurance, investment banking and stock market/financial analysis work, and also for those jobs requiring strong communication skills.

The Higher Education Statistics Agency (HESA) provides detailed analysis of careers entered by graduates in different subjects from data supplied to them by universities and colleges. The figures are for 2000, the latest year for which information is available, and show that:

★ 60 entered the occupational category **Managers and Administrators**.
  Of these, 30 were specialist managers; 10 were managers and administrators 'not elsewhere classified'.
★ 50 entered **Professional Occupations**.
  20 went into teaching; 20 into business and finance and 10 into librarianship and related professions.
★ 60 entered **Associate Professional and Technical Occupations**.
  10 as business and finance associate professionals; 30 as literary, artistic and sports associate professionals.
★ 90 entered **Clerical and Secretarial Occupations**.
  10 as numerical clerks and cashiers; 30 into general clerical work and 20 as secretaries and personal assistants.
★ 20 entered **Personal and Protective Service**.
  Of these, 10 went into catering.
★ 30 entered **Sales and Related Occupations**.

(Total number of students surveyed = 320.)

NB. The HESA figures are for students who graduated in 1999/2000.

All figures relate to graduates who went straight into employment. They do not include those doing postgraduate courses.

And these figures should be treated with caution. Compiled six months after students have graduated, they are bound to include some who are in temporary jobs to gain experience or to earn a living while making applications for 'graduate-level' jobs. If asked their whereabouts six months after graduating both Tim Youngs and Rebecca Hon, for example (see page 78 and below), would have given their destinations as 'Clerical', whereas both used those jobs as stepping stones to satisfying careers.

The graduates whose case studies follow have used their skills to enter very different careers.

Rebecca Hon
Human Resources Officer, HFC Bank

A-levels: French, German, Classical Civilisation, General Studies. A/S Maths.
Degree: Classical Civilisation (2:1), University of Birmingham.

Rebecca's interest in classical languages and civilisation came about almost by accident. At the GCSE stage she was keen to pursue a course in modern languages and eventually work abroad. Thinking that a knowledge of Latin would be useful to a more in-depth study of modern languages, she persuaded one of her teachers to give her lessons after school. When she transferred to sixth form college she started A-level Classical Civilisation – *and* took GCSEs in both Latin and Greek.

> 'I became hooked! I loved all the study of ancient civilisations and the two literatures. Right until the final moment of filling in my UCAS form I was torn between classics or modern languages. I nearly applied for joint French and Classical

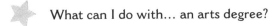

Civilisation. Dropping the French was very much a last-minute decision.

'Several people asked why I was doing dead subjects, but I had no particular career in mind so I couldn't see the point of doing anything supposedly more "useful" and my parents, who had always been very keen on the idea of education for its own sake, were very encouraging.

'As I didn't have A-levels in Greek or Latin I took the civilisation course instead of straight Classics. My course was composed of 25% Latin, 25% Greek and the remainder covered art, literature, history, politics and mythology. It was a wonderful course. I loved the breadth and the fact that I was studying two civilisations from every perspective – cultural, religious, political …

'At the end of my second year I obtained a grant to do a four-week study tour in Greece and Italy. I went with two friends from the course and we worked really, really hard but enjoyed every moment. We visited 12 archaeological sites and 13 museums – then spent the last few days relaxing in Paris on the way back. I used the tour as a basis for my dissertation, which was on the existence of politics in art and how art can be used as propaganda.'

Rebecca postponed all thoughts of careers until well after finals. She had worked through most of her time at Birmingham in the HFC call centre, processing loan applications, and had been promoted to supervisory level. She now went to work there full time to give herself a breathing space. Then came the offer of a six-month secondment to work as a training officer in the Human Resources (HR) Department. She had done some staff training in the call centre so accepted the offer and became very interested in other aspects of HR work. She stayed on in the department when offered a permanent post and now does a combination of training, recruitment and administrative work.

'I manage the department's administration with two assistants. We are responsible for all the "new starter" administration, making sure that we have checked references – you have to be very careful in a bank – see that contracts of employment are issued and do the paperwork required for people to get paid! I support the call centre managers in their recruitment with advertising and interviewing. I have to make sure that they don't infringe any aspects of employment law when they interview. If a manager asked a question or made any remark that could be construed as discriminatory we could be in trouble.

'I run one-day induction programmes for new employees, when I give presentations on the company and its work, their responsibilities, rights and benefits, and I take them on tours of the premises. I am also the nominated HR representative for Credit Services, my old department of 350 people. This means that if anyone there has a grievance or problem they can come to discuss it with me as their first point of contact. I sometimes get people complaining about their managers and I have to be diplomatic. Quite often I find myself agreeing with the manager – if someone has been warned about too many unexplained absences for instance – and I have to tell them so. Learning to tell people off has been difficult for me. I prefer the "pat on the back" approach.

'Something else that I have found slightly difficult is the content of some of the professional exams I am working for. I am doing Chartered Institute of Personnel and Development exams. It takes three years – of about eight hours' study a week. The material is very different from anything I have studied before. There are far more facts and figures and everything is presented in a business format. On the whole though, human resources work is very enjoyable and it's almost as varied as my degree course.'

Skills Rebecca gained on her degree course ...

★ Time management: 'I only had about eight hours' lectures a week. In my first year I wasn't at all organised. Then I started to acquire some self-discipline.'
★ Ability to look at things from all angles: 'Sometimes I feel as though I am being pulled in two different directions by management and employees and by the fact that human resources does not equate to social work. The company has to make a profit.'
★ 'Enjoyment of working on lots of different topics.'

... and from student life in general

★ Teamwork – from the study tour.
★ Negotiating skills – 'from sharing a house and arguing over the shopping and washing up'.
★ Time management again – from working part time in the second and third years.

Rebecca's Advice
'Do a subject you enjoy. My strongest advice however would be to get some work experience – any kind. It doesn't really matter. When I look at some application forms I am horrified to find that some students have never had a job at all. They have no appreciation of the world of work.'

Career note
Human resources or personnel managers may specialise in recruitment, training, employment legislation, strategic planning, industrial relations or, in some companies, perform two or more of these functions. Some large organisations recruit graduates directly on to training programmes in HR work. Other routes are to get a foothold in an organisation as Rebecca did and move to the Human Resources Department when a vacancy arises, or take a postgraduate diploma course in HR management as a first step.

Gaining membership of the Chartered Institute of Personnel and Development is not obligatory but most employers expect their HR staff to do so. Study for the examinations can be done through evening classes, day release or distance learning.

Tom Broadhurst
Chartered Accountant, PriceWaterhouseCoopers

A-levels: Latin, Greek, Maths.
Degree: Classics (2:1), University of Durham

Tom did not go straight to university after A-levels but took a gap year, during which he did a French language course in France, had several temporary jobs in Paris and spent three months working on a kibbutz in Israel. He then went to

Durham to take up his place to read Greek and Roman Studies. Why that course?

'It was a way of combining my favourite A-level subjects. I liked both languages – Latin slightly more than Greek. They continued to interest me at degree level. I enjoyed the language study, the logic and mental exercise of doing translation work and getting it to make sense. I also enjoyed the literature – there can't be much of Virgil and Homer that I haven't read – and the literary criticism that was part of the course.'

Latin and Greek may seem irrelevant to some people. What reaction did Tom have to his intention of doing them to degree level?

'Some people laughed! My teachers said they were my strongest subjects, therefore it would be better to continue with them. My father was very encouraging. He said that as there were not so many courses in classics I would be different and have rarity value when it came to looking for a job.'

Tom had no idea about a future career when he applied for his degree course. He did, though, start to consider the question seriously quite early on his course. During his first year he made some preliminary investigations and decided that a financial or legal career, preferably in the City, would interest him. He found out that he would need a professional qualification after his degree – in law or in one of the branches of finance. Law would involve further full-time study. Accountancy, he discovered, offered the opportunity to train while in employment.

Towards the end of his first year he attended some presentations from major employers who visited the university and heard about the possibility of doing a summer vacation placement or internship. He then went to spend his second year at the University of Liège in Belgium, under the ERASMUS programme, where he continued to study classics – in French. *'It was a challenge, but I soon became able to cope with taking down lecture notes in French. Thirty-minute oral examinations were something else!'*

By then, Tom had decided to find out what was involved in accountancy and wrote from Liège to several major firms in London. He was accepted to do a vacation placement with PriceWaterhouseCoopers and worked there on his return. The scheme was very well organised, Tom worked in personal and corporate tax departments where he was given real work to do – '*I went from knowing nothing to knowing quite a lot by the end of the summer*' – and attended several short management courses. At the end of the placement he applied to join the firm. He did not find the selection process, consisting of group exercises with other applicants and interviews with partners, too difficult, given his experience, and he returned for his final year with a job offer under his belt.

Trainee accountants (known as students) have to study for professional examinations. Anyone thinking that they have said 'Goodbye' to examinations after graduation can find this a shock to the system. For six months Tom spent one week in four at a tutorial centre. At the end of that period came the first exam – and any student who failed would have been instantly dismissed. The pressure was on and Tom often had to work in the evenings, after a day in the office, when all he wanted to do was '*kick my shoes off and flop in front of the TV*'. He 'scraped through' and went on to complete his three-year training period. In his second and third years he continued to learn the work of the taxation departments and spent 12 weeks in each year at the tutorial centre – '*just like a university term*'.

Tom has recently qualified and provides information on clients' tax matters for different audit* teams within the firm. Some of this comes from clients' records, some he requests by letter, and he spends some of his time visiting clients at their premises and asking for the information he needs from their own internal accountants.

---

* Audit. Limited companies are legally obliged to have an annual assessment of their financial state conducted by external auditors, who attest that their accounts show a true and fair picture of their financial position. This is attached to the accounts that go to the Inland Revenue.

What sort of skills should a good accountant possess?

According to Tom:

★ Patience.
★ The ability to pay attention to detail: 'The firm could be sued over mistakes.'
★ A sense of humour! 'Some of the work is mundane, but we joke a lot. Most people here are very witty.'
★ Strong communication skills: 'You are working in new teams and with new clients all the time.'
★ The ability to get on with a job very quickly. 'Clients are charged for the amount of time we work.' (Tom has to record his work on a computer system so that clients can be charged for six-minute periods.)

The skills Tom gained from his degree ...

★ Self-discipline.
★ Ability to reason logically. (Classical languages are very structured.)
★ Ability to pay attention to detail – from translation work.

... and from university life in general

★ Ability to form relationships with new people – from very different backgrounds.
★ Teamwork (from playing hockey for his college).
★ Confidence – particularly from the ERASMUS and gap years.

Tom's advice

'You are going to spend three years of your life at university, so make sure that you do something you will enjoy. Employers don't attach much importance to the actual subject. It is an advantage for a graduate going into a career such as mine to be able to demonstrate relevant skills and experience. If you get the opportunity to do a vacation scheme placement as I did, go for it. Be prepared to continue studying after you have graduated in order to obtain professional qualifications – and to give up some of your spare time to do so.'

Career note

Most chartered accountants train *in practice* – which means with a firm of accountants approved to offer training by one of the Institutes of Chartered Accountants (ICA – for England and Wales, Scotland or Ireland.) It is also possible to train in certain approved organisations in industry, commerce and the public sector.

In England and Wales over 90% of entrants are graduates.

Once qualified, chartered accountants may work in practice – as most choose to do – or in one of the other sectors. Other forms of accountancy are public sector and management accountancy. Graduates in any discipline can enter any form of accountancy and train in employment for qualifications of the ICA, Association of Chartered Certified Accountants, Chartered Institute of Management Accountants or Chartered Institute of Public Finance Accountancy.

English 4

All English graduates go into teaching, librarianship, publishing or journalism. Right? Wrong. They are certainly fairly obvious follow-ons from an English degree, and are particularly popular with English graduates, but there would not be enough jobs to go round if every student wanted one of these careers. Many do – and some are disappointed every year. They have to choose alternatives. Other students look into alternatives from the start.

What will you gain from doing an English degree? Like the classicists you will find that there is little demand for your specialist literary knowledge outside academic and creative employment. However, you should emerge from your degree course equipped to read widely and pick out the information essential to the job in hand, also to argue a case clearly and with conviction. There are no right and wrong answers where this subject is concerned so you will learn to weigh up the merits of different arguments and put forward the best (or some of the best) – a useful skill in many managerial jobs or in those involving strategic planning where the best possible or compromise solutions to problems are required. You will also be an excellent communicator and presenter of material.

So English *can* lead to teaching (including teaching English as a foreign language), publishing, librarianship and journalism. It can be extremely useful in advertising and public relations work where creative text has to be produced. Many editors, copywriters, journalists and PR executives have backgrounds in English. (Others do not.) It is also useful in broadcasting.

This does not mean that English graduates can do only creative jobs. Two of the case studies that follow show them working in very technical areas of employment.

An annual survey of graduate destinations is carried out by the Association of Graduate Careers Advisory Services for publication in a booklet, *What do Graduates do?* In this publication detailed information is given for three of our six subjects, English being one of them. Careers entered are grouped under occupational headings with examples of specific jobs and employers being quoted in some of these. It shows that by far the largest number enter administrative work, followed by commercial, industrial and public sector management. (This category includes HM Forces – since officers are leaders and managers – but is not necessarily everyone's idea of a management job!). Next comes retailing and hospitality, followed by media and literary professions – quite low down the list. Marketing, advertising, sales and PR form the next category of any size.

Possibly surprising occupations include accountancy, insurance brokerage, health promotion and recruitment consultancy.

The more detailed HESA breakdown of the destinations of English graduates shows that:

★ 660 entered the occupational category **Managers and Administrators.**
  Of these, 20 were in national and local government, large companies and organisations; 270 were specialist managers; 70 were financial institution and office managers or Civil Service executive officers; 100 were managers and proprietors in service industries; 170 were managers and administrators 'not elsewhere classified'.
★ 310 entered **Professional Occupations**.
  210 went into teaching; 60 into business and finance; 20 into librarianship and related professions.
★ 590 entered **Associate Professional and Technical Occupations**.
  30 as computer analysts and programmers; 10 as health associate professionals; 90 as business and finance

associate professionals; 50 as social welfare associate professionals; 320 as literary, artistic and sports associate professionals.

★ 810 entered **Clerical and Secretarial Occupations**.
60 in the Civil Service and local government; 80 as numerical clerks and cashiers; 100 as filing and records clerks; 360 into general clerical work; 100 as secretaries and personal assistants; 60 as receptionists.

★ 210 entered **Personal and Protective Service**.
10 into security and protective service; 80 into catering; 20 into health and related occupations; 80 into childcare and related occupations.

★ 340 entered S**ales and Related Occupations**.
10 as buyers, brokers and related agents; 50 as sales representatives; 240 as sales assistants.

(Total number of students surveyed = 3030.)

NB. The *What do Graduates do?* information refers to 1999 graduates. The new edition was due out very shortly after this book was written. HESA figures are for students who graduated in 1999/2000.

All figures relate to graduates who went straight into employment. They do not include those doing postgraduate courses.

And these figures should be treated with caution. Compiled six months after students have graduated, they are bound to include some who are in temporary jobs to gain experience or to earn a living while making applications for 'graduate-level' jobs. If asked their whereabouts six months after graduating both Tim Youngs and Rebecca Hon, for example (see pp 78 and 29), would have given their destinations as 'Clerical', whereas both used those jobs as stepping stones to satisfying careers.

Katie Flanagan
Web Consultant, Hampshire County Council

A-levels: English, Maths, Music.
Degree: English (2:1), Royal Holloway, University of London.

Katie had a difficult choice to make, between English and music, for her degree course. She loved English at A-level and felt that it was her strongest subject. She also loved music. In the end she reasoned that music was almost a vocational subject – and she wanted something more academic. She also realised that she could keep up her music as a spare-time activity. So, English it was. At that point her future plans were not decided but she was thinking about either a higher degree in English followed by an academic career, work in publishing or returning to music.

At university she had the opportunity to develop her singing ability. She joined the college chapel choir and spent around seven hours each week rehearsing, performing and taking singing lessons. (The choir sang in the chapel for 15 minutes every morning and at evensong on Thursdays and Sundays.)

Katie made use of her careers advisory service in good time. She attended some general careers information sessions and others on different occupational areas, went to skills workshops on CV preparation and interview technique, read widely in the careers information room – and finally had two one-to-one consultations with a careers adviser. It was during the second meeting that information technology was suggested.

> 'I asked about publishing and was told that it was very competitive. The adviser suggested librarianship – which didn't interest me. Then she mentioned IT. I was daunted by the fact that I had no technical knowledge, but she said that I had a very good combination of skills from my degree subject and from my music and maths A-levels and that many employers did not require specific degrees. (I found that to be very true when I joined Hampshire County Council. They take students from all subjects – and actually prefer to have some non-IT graduates.)'

Katie attended a selection process lasting a whole day.

'I had to do some aptitude tests – which were obviously devised to assess logical ability – then attend two interviews. The second, with two people, was very searching. They asked questions on my dissertation (on Milton) and asked me what general skills I thought I had. I mentioned analysis, communication and time management. Then they asked what I thought my weaknesses were! I said that I seemed to be the only undergraduate present – all the other applicants were already working – and that I had no IT expertise. In other words was I too young and inexperienced? They said "No," and explained that I could be trained on the technical side. They wanted flexible people who were good all-rounders.'

Katie's job is very wide ranging.

'It's very diverse but the main focus is Web work. I attended some courses – mainly on business skills and project management skills. I largely taught myself HTML and Web design work! I studied in quiet periods at work and sometimes at home. That is where the discipline of managing my own work and my research skills came in useful.

'My department does work for other departments in the Council and also for some external clients such as the police force. It could be a question of designing a small website or a really major project like one I have worked on for an external client – the Road Casualty Reduction Group for the South East. If it is a small job I do it all myself; a bigger one is done by a team. For instance when we had a 600-page website for a local transport plan three of us divided the work under chapter headings and took sections each.

'I have now been promoted and a lot of my work consists of project management. When a client contacts the department with a request I do the initial liaison. I set up a meeting, establish exactly what they require, then write a proposal and work out the cost. If the client accepts, I allocate work to other Web designers and give them a full brief. I usually leave further liaison with the client up to them but I keep a watchful eye on the timescale and costs during the project. I often have several projects to manage and have to be good at moving from one to another. I enjoy that!'

Katie is now moving back to her original idea of a musical career. She has negotiated a part-time contract with her employers, works for them three days a week and spends the other two having her voice trained professionally at Trinity College of Music in London.

The skills Katie gained from her degree ...

★ Analytical ability.
★ Communication: 'My ability in English is used all the time as I write a lot of proposals, reports and feasibility studies.'
★ Discussion: listening to other people's points of view.

... and from student life in general

★ Time management (balancing academic work with choir commitments).
★ Teamwork.
★ Customer service skills from part-time work as a waitress.
★ Responsibility through part-time work childminding.

Katie's advice

'Do a subject you enjoy. You will do well if you really like it. One of my friends started a degree in classics and dropped out. He switched to linguistics, which he did like – and got a First! Do think about careers and career choice – but leave the actual jobhunt until after finals in order to concentrate on academic work. (*But* be aware that some companies have early closing dates – which would mean an earlier application if you were interested in them.)'

Career note

Arts graduates enter several career areas connected with computing and information technology – programming, systems analysis, software engineering, network administration and Web design. Some, like Katie, train in employment. Others take a postgraduate diploma course first.

Paul Ayers
Account Executive, Giga Information Group

A-levels: English Literature, History, Economics.
Degree: English Literature with Subsidiary Political Philosophy (2:1), University of Birmingham.

Paul's current job is with an IT advisory firm that provides specialist supplies and research in the IT field to large corporations. '*It is rather like producing* Which Mortgage? *or* What Car? *magazines – except that we go one stage deeper and provide custom-made research and in-depth advice for particular clients*.' As an account executive he provides support to an account manager. His job is to facilitate – to pull various strands together and ensure that clients get the best solution to their problem.

Before taking up his present job a year ago Paul spent five years in the Royal Navy. He had known that he wanted to join the Navy from an early age and had held a naval scholarship throughout his A-level course. He then applied successfully for a university cadetship and attended university as a serving naval officer, having first completed officer training at Dartmouth. He wore his uniform only on formal occasions – 'It was very good for balls!' – and for graduation. He was visited once a term by a naval officer who checked on his progress, and was required to join the Royal Naval Volunteer Reserve along with 14 other officer cadets in the West Midlands area. He spent part of his vacations doing naval courses or sea training but still found time to do some part-time work in a pub.

The Royal Navy left the choice of degree subject up to Paul, except for the proviso that it must be in an academic subject:

> 'They want graduates among the officers who can hold their own in discussions and conversations with the people they will meet during their careers – and, very important, those who can present well-argued cases when it comes to fighting the Navy's corner in issues such as staffing, budgets or defence cuts.'

So why did Paul choose English?

'For pure pleasure. I wanted to get my teeth into something and enjoy it for its own sake. Yes, I could spend two hours dissecting a Keats poem but I would be enjoying it at the same time. There are no right answers in literature. It always leads to wider debate.'

The 20% of Paul's course taken up by political philosophy was less good: '*It was disappointing. I felt that we were largely learning what other people thought rather than coming to conclusions for ourselves.*'

After graduating Paul continued his professional training to be an executive officer (formerly known as seaman officer). He spent eight months working in all departments of a ship, even in the stores and bakery, in order to experience every facet of life on board and to gain an appreciation of the work done by every single officer and rating. This period was followed by a shore-based Officer of the Watch course. Officers of the Watch are the Navy's navigating officers. The course was technical, but Paul did not find it difficult – '*although I did need everything I had learned in GCSE maths.*'

Then came four very full years spent mainly at sea, on different ships. Paul took part in minesweeping duties, fisheries protection, official visits to several US ports, NATO exercises, and saw active service in Sierra Leone. In addition to driving the ship for eight- or ten-hour shifts each day his duties included preparing navigational charts and pilotage plans for the next passage (while keeping a watchful eye on the weather) and keeping a detailed ship's log, which included details of every activity undertaken each day. This had to be kept meticulously as it could be subpoenaed at any time by parliamentary committees or by the courts. (Paul also had to appear as an expert witness in court from time to time – for example in cases where foreign trawlers were disputing the Navy's right to board them by claiming to be outside territorial waters.) He was also the communications officer, issuing codes for radio signals back to the UK and to other ships and writing signals for warfare exercises. On top of all that he kept the accounts for all official entertainment on board and was responsible for the welfare, discipline and career development of 15 ratings. More court appearances! Paul occasionally had to defend his men in courts martial.

After four years at sea the job was becoming too stressful, he was disillusioned by the defence cuts taking place – and he left to jobhunt as a civilian. He was fairly soon offered jobs as a project manager by companies that valued the experience he had gained as an officer, but decided to take up the offer of a job in Giga's sales department. From there he moved to an accounts management team – which he much preferred to sales – and on to his current position.

Skills Paul gained from the course

★ Presentation skills.
★ The ability to read behind the lines and establish what is really meant – 'a useful tool when arguing with civil servants in Whitehall.'
★ 'I had the leadership and teamwork skills necessary for a naval officer already – either naturally or developed at Dartmouth. However, I think studying literature taught me to be better at thinking things through – and to see other people's point of view, something that the officer training does not bring out.'

Paul's advice

'Do a subject for pleasure. The opportunity to spend so much time with like minds is something that will never come again. We would often come out of a seminar and continue the discussion over coffee. Employers will value you as a person.'

Career note

Arts graduates can enter the Royal Navy as officers in the following specialisms: Warfare (which includes navigation, air traffic and fighter control, and aircrew work); and Supply (administration, logistics, stores and accounting). Women may not serve in submarines or in mine warfare and clearance diving.

Officer opportunities are also available in the Royal Marines, Army and Royal Air Force.

Each of the services offers two forms of financial support to degree course students: cadetship, which is what Paul had, and bursary. (Under the bursary scheme students remain civilians.) It is not necessary however to have either. Many graduate officer entrants decide to join during their time in higher education.

Rowena Wisniewska
Assistant Solicitor, Pitmans, Reading

A-levels: English, German, Art; English S-level.
Degree: English Literature (2:1), University of York. Plus two years' postgraduate study in law.

Rowena chose her degree subject after debating for some time between English and German, having decided art was not sufficiently academic. She was enjoying both the other subjects equally but finally selected English because it was her best subject. She had no career plans at that time but was thinking in terms of postgraduate work, possibly to MA or PhD level.

She thoroughly enjoyed her degree course and knew that she had made the right choice. Chaucer was of particular interest – *'If I had followed through the idea of doing an MA it would have been on Chaucer.'* She did not mind having to learn Anglo-Saxon as part of the course. Having German A-level meant that she was confident of her linguistic ability.

Rowena made full use of her time at York. From her first year she did voluntary work for Nightline, a confidential telephone counselling service. She received full training for the work and was required to be on duty overnight on a rota basis several nights each term.

'On some nights you could sleep but on others the phone might go constantly. It was very challenging as I never knew who was at the end of the phone or what problem they would want to talk about. I very quickly learned to think on my feet and respond. Some people were very upset and needed a listening ear. A few could be quite aggressive and rude. I developed so many skills from that work – communication skills obviously – also how to empathise with distressed people and learn not to take things personally. Sometimes, for instance, I would think that I had not helped the caller at all. (At others there was a good feeling from having been of some use.) I also gained a better understanding of different people and of a wider society. I put Nightline down on application forms for my postgraduate training and for jobs – and that was the thing that I was asked about most often at interviews.'

Rowena also co-edited an arts magazine with a friend. They selected poetry and prose written by student contributors, and helped to produce the magazine, which was sold on campus and through a major bookshop. Although the two were good friends they did not always see eye to eye on matters editorial. Training in negotiating skills!

During her second year Rowena saw some information on conversion courses for graduates in subjects other than law who wanted to become solicitors. Until that point she had not realised that such a route was possible. *'I thought it would have been necessary to have a law degree.'* She was beginning to consider some kind of career which would enable her to work directly in the community and she realised that she could do so by working as a solicitor. She stayed on in York, where there is a branch of the College of Law, to do two courses – at a cost of £5,500 (plus living expenses) each year. She financed the courses through loans, assistance from her father and by working in the summer vacations in a plastics factory.

The first course, leading to the Common Professional Examination (see p. 49) was very hard work – *'teaching us almost everything that is included on a law degree!'* There were seven exams one after another towards the end and most students were working until 10pm. The second course concentrated more on the skills needed by lawyers and that, too, was hard work.

After the courses came two years of salaried training with a solicitor under a *training contract*. Rowena spent this with a firm of solicitors in Reading. It was something of a shock as it was the first office-based job she had ever had. All her part-time student work had been in factories, fast food outlets and restaurants. She gained good all-round experience and particularly enjoyed court work. Even if she had not stayed in law, she says, the practice in interviewing clients and the knowledge of court procedures would have stood her in good stead for other community-based careers.

She has very recently qualified as a solicitor and has started a new job with a large practice in Reading where she will be specialising in civil litigation. At first she will work with other solicitors engaged on big cases and will do research for small portions of the work. In time she will build up a list of her own clients.

What skills does a good solicitor need?
According to Rowena:

★ Communication.
★ Ability to get on with people – of all backgrounds and temperaments, especially when they are angry and distressed.
★ Diplomacy – but combined with the skill of knowing when to be firm and when to insist.
★ Judgement: 'You need to be a good judge of character and to know when people are telling the truth.'
★ Approachability.
★ Stamina: 'You have to carry on and give matters your full attention even when you have been working hard and are tired.'

The skills Rowena gained from her degree course ...

★ The ability to assimilate and evaluate large amounts of information.
★ Skill in forming judgements and opinions.
★ Writing skill: 'very important in legal drafting'.

... and from university life in general

'All the skills I gained from Nightline work – which also helped me to develop as a person and increased my confidence.'

Rowena's advice

'I wouldn't do anything differently. I could have saved a year by doing a law degree. But I had no career plans at that point. Also, I wouldn't have missed the experience of reading English for anything. You should think very carefully about the financial aspect of doing two postgraduate courses though. The cost of doing that added to the debt that students build up these days on a first-degree course is considerable.'

(Rowena graduated just before tuition fees were introduced.)

Career note
Non-law graduates who decide to become either barristers or solicitors must take further courses. Both barristers and

solicitors first take the Common Professional Examination (CPE) or Postgraduate Diploma in Law course (one year full time or two years part time). This is followed for barristers by the Bar Vocational course and for solicitors by the Legal Practice course – again, over one year full time or two part time. Barristers then do one year's pupillage; solicitors a two-year training contract.

Some large law firms sponsor students through the CPE and diploma courses but competition to join such firms is severe.

The above applies to England and Wales. The system is different in Scotland, where entrants to either branch of the profession must have degrees in Scottish law from Scottish universities *or* undertake a very lengthy conversion training.

5   History

History graduates have some fairly obvious careers to consider, namely teacher, archivist, museum curator and librarian. These make direct use of the subject. But dozens choose alternative careers, many of which are totally unrelated to history.

What skills will you gain from doing history? Understanding and analysing issues are major ones. You will also learn to put forward ideas and arguments clearly, while the ability to read widely, deal with vast amounts of information and pick out the relevant are skills familiar to all historians. Students frequently refer to the sheer mass of material they must sift through in order to write just one essay. (Careers that make use of these skills very heavily include law, journalism, local government administration, and high-level work in the Civil Service – helping to formulate policy and advising ministers.) You will be able to organise facts logically and to condense material and write concisely – a very useful ability in many jobs that call for the preparation of written reports or the giving of oral briefings or presentations (from sales pitches in an advertising agency to a report on a potential company for takeover in investment banking).

The publication *What do Graduates do?* covers history in its annual survey of students graduating in different subjects. It shows that the largest number found administrative or managerial work in both the public and private sectors. Next come retailing and hospitality work, then the category 'Other professional occupations', which includes law, followed by business and finance, advertising and public relations.

The surprises are that nearly 6% are in business and financial work, including accountancy; 11% entered retailing and hospitality work.

Among specific examples of 'unusual' jobs are:

★ Army officer
★ Business travel consultant
★ Editorial assistant on a computer magazine
★ IT consultant
★ Management trainee with a fast-food firm
★ RAF pilot
★ Software developer
★ Teacher of English as a foreign language
★ Youth worker.

HESA statistics show that:

★ 580 entered the occupational category **Managers and Administrators**.
   Of these, 20 were in national and local government, large companies and organisations; 200 were specialist managers; 70 were financial institution and office managers or Civil Service executive officers; 10 were managers in transport and storing; 100 were managers and proprietors in service industries; 160 were managers and administrators 'not elsewhere classified'.
★ 280 entered **Professional Occupations**.
   100 went into teaching; 100 into business and finance; 40 into librarianship and related professions.
★ 350 entered **Associate Professional and Technical Occupations**.
   20 as computer analysts and programmers; 110 as business and finance associate professionals; 40 as social welfare associate professionals; 100 as literary, artistic and sports associate professionals.
★ 710 entered **Clerical and Secretarial Occupations**.
   70 in the Civil Service and local government; 110 as numerical clerks and cashiers; 90 as filing and records clerks; 260 into general clerical work; 80 as secretaries and personal assistants; 50 as receptionists.

★ 150 entered **Personal and Protective Service**.
20 went into security and protective service; 50 into
catering; 20 into health and related occupations; 50 into
childcare and related occupations.
★ 260 entered S**ales and Related Occupations**.
30 as sales representatives; 190 as sales assistants.

(Total number of students surveyed = 2450.)

NB. The W*hat do Graduates do?* information refers to 1999
graduates. The new edition was due out very shortly after this
book was written. HESA figures are for students who
graduated in 1999/2000.

All figures relate to graduates who went straight into
employment. They do not include those doing postgraduate
courses.

And these figures should be treated with caution. Compiled
six months after students have graduated, they are bound to
include some who are in temporary jobs to gain experience or
to earn a living while making applications for 'graduate-level'
jobs. If asked their whereabouts six months after graduating
both Tim Youngs and Rebecca Hon, for example (see pp 78
and 29), would have given their destinations as 'Clerical',
whereas both used those jobs as stepping stones to satisfying
careers.

The three people featured in the case studies that follow have
used the analytical and communication skills they acquired
through studying history in very different jobs.

Michael van der Beugel
Investment Banking Analyst, Credit Suisse First Boston

A-levels: History, German, Maths. A/S Further Maths,
Philosophy.
Degree: History (2:1), University of Edinburgh.

The bank where Michael works handles, among other things, company mergers and acquisitions. There are two strands to his job:

'Our aim is to get business from the top blue-chip companies. One of my roles is to help my managing director get a mandate – by writing a proposal, which is basically a marketing brief, setting out information for a potential client, explaining how experienced the bank is in this kind of work, how well we know the sector and how many similar transactions we have previously managed. So I do the research and prepare material that will be used in a client presentation.

'The second aspect concerns execution. When the bank has won some new business we help the client to achieve their objective. Suppose a company is offering itself for a merger. Other companies – prospective buyers – need as much information as possible on the first company. I get all the relevant information on its performance, current situation and future potential – with the aim of getting as good a price as possible and achieving maximum value for its shareholders. Detailed reports using some of my research are in due course sent out to interested parties. When bids are made they come through the bank. We assess them, whittle them down and get the best price on the table. The administrative work then begins. Our role is to create the forum in which accountants and lawyers can work together successfully to achieve the sale and purchase. We also have to keep a watchful eye to ensure that takeover rules are strictly adhered to. Any bank that failed to do so would never get business again!'

One thing Michael has had to come to terms with is that it is perfectly possible to spend days or weeks preparing a beautifully argued case and then see the work totally rejected if his managers decided not to pursue that line of business or if a rival bank successfully bids for the work. But this is not uncommon in many graduate jobs in the City or indeed in marketing, PR etc.

Other than research skills and the ability to cope with disappointment what skills does his work require?

53

'You must certainly not be a clock watcher! In investment banks people often have to work late into the night when a merger or takeover is at a crucial stage. To work a 120-hour week is not uncommon then. You need real commitment, stamina – and any personal relationship must be strong to survive. All you want to do at weekends is sleep. You need to be able to juggle different commitments and prioritise. For example, I might be working with a newspaper and media team one day and with an oil or gas team the next. I could be working simultaneously on several tasks for each team. You must do everything that you promise to do. We are always deadline driven. We cannot cope with one person turning up to a meeting with the managing director with a piece of work not done. (You soon have to learn to be assertive too – able to say "No" when you are being asked to work to a totally unrealistic timescale!)

'While studying history did not prepare me directly for this type of work it gave me a good academic grounding and developed my intellectual ability. I need to be able to grasp facts quickly, take in huge amounts of information – and think quickly.'

Michael had no firm idea about a future career when he applied for his degree course, although as a result of some gap year experience banking was always at the back of his mind. The gap year had not been in Michael's original planning. He applied initially for law but, as he now says, his heart was not in it; he did not put in a very strong application form – and was not offered any places. The second time around he chose a subject for pure enjoyment, knowing that it could eventually lead him in several different directions. In the gap year he travelled in the USA and spent four months working in a bank in Frankfurt to improve his German. *It wasn't a very well-structured piece of work experience but at least I got to see a trading floor – and it looked good on my CV when I was applying for this job.'*

By the beginning of his final year he had decided on investment banking and made six or seven applications, after attending presentations at the university from recruiters. Job applications then became very time consuming – he was interviewed by four banks, which unfortunately coincided with the time he had allocated to writing his dissertation. Credit Suisse First Boston initially interviewed him in Edinburgh, then flew him down to London one Saturday, when he had individual interviews with seven department managers: *'It was quite hard going by the seventh!'*

The skills Michael gained from his degree ...

★ Analytical skill: 'the ability to reason why something happened, not simply reproduce a list of facts. You can transfer this skill to dealing with different situations. Studying history teaches you to look for the holes in an argument. You soon see when someone is trying to pull the wool over your eyes!'
★ Ability to be focused on a task: 'usually an essay'.
★ Time management and the ability to meet a deadline: 'I wasn't the greatest at time management but I always met essay deadlines, even if I had to work until 5am.'

... and from university life in general

★ Ability to form relationships with different personalities.
★ Capacity for hard work: 'One summer I worked as a crew mate on a Dutch vessel. The work was hard and the hours very long – good training for this job.'
★ Confidence: particularly from the periods spent in living in different countries: 'I was on my own two feet, particularly in Frankfurt – and learned not to moan when things didn't go quite right.'
★ Teamwork: 'from playing rugby. A lot of people in the City are rugby players, so there must be something in it!'

Michael's advice

'Do the subject you want to do. Luckily, UK employers still recognise the value of non-specific degrees. Several students of other nationalities who came to work here when I did had degrees in corporate finance economics or business studies and had impressive CVs. Interestingly, some of them have long since departed. However, do be aware of the competition for jobs (especially from multi-lingual foreign students) and be ready to put extra things on your CV to get yourself noticed. It would be a good idea to do a vacation internship.'

Career note

Investment banks recruit graduates from all disciplines. Starting salaries are among the highest on offer but the total number of trainees required in any one year is comparatively small. Entry is therefore highly competitive. Banks train their own staff internally. Some run training programmes of up to two years during which time graduates spend periods of several months in different departments, while others recruit to specific departments and have shorter training periods. Investment banks do not normally make use of the Chartered Institute of Bankers' (CIOB) examinations but use those of the Securities Institute instead.

The retail (high street) banks and mortgage banks (former building societies) plus the remaining building societies all recruit graduates in any subject for branch or specialised management work. Entrants to these banks are normally expected to achieve the CIOB qualifications in a specified period.

Nicholas Chalmers
Revenue Manager, Landmark Hotel, London

A-levels: History, French, English.
Degree: Modern History and International Relations (2:1), University of Reading. MSc in International Hotel Management, University of Surrey.

Nicholas's present job involves maximising the hotel's profit. He has to try to ensure a high room occupancy rate – making the crucial decision whether and when to reduce prices – and works closely with the sales and marketing team and with the food and beverage manager over banquets and functions.

'In this present job I am less people oriented than when I was working front of house. Now I need to be more analytical and able to handle graphs and charts – examine them carefully and work out trends from them. I then have to make strategic decisions based on these results and be able to justify what I do. It's a question of being able to look at a problem from all angles – then come down on one side. I still need communication skills. Now I have to be able to explain and justify my decisions to colleagues, many of whom are not too happy with figures! In previous jobs it was more a case of being able to explain that I want something done in a certain way and why.'

Nicholas previously worked at the Royal Crescent Hotel in Bath as a reservations manager and front of house manager before gaining promotion to deputy general manager. The move to London was in order to experience work in a different type of hotel. (The Landmark has mainly corporate clients.) He was until recently an assistant general manager there. His present job, he says, is part of a deliberate plan to gain experience in different types of work.

Why did he decide on hotel management while doing a history degree?

'Because I really enjoyed short-term jobs I had in hotels. I worked as a waiter at the Royal Crescent in my home town of Bath between finishing my A-levels and starting my course at Reading. Hotel work was an obvious area of temporary jobs in Bath. I liked it so much that I worked there during every vacation. As I was coming to the end of my degree course and beginning to think seriously about careers I suddenly thought, "Why not do this as a profession?" I then decided to get a respected qualification behind me. I knew that some hotel chains did training programmes from students in non-related disciplines but I wanted to get a grounding in both the theory and practice of management first and put myself on an equal footing with applicants from the best professional courses.'

So Nicholas applied to one of the most highly regarded courses, the Master's at Surrey. *'It is quite rare to hold an MSc in the hotel business and I knew that with it I would be able to progress quickly.'* He was slightly surprised to be accepted since the usual requirement for entry was a first degree in hotel management or substantial managerial experience in a hotel. The course was excellent. He gained a grounding in budgeting, marketing, finance and tourism. More important was the chance to network with and learn from other students. There were 140 in all doing hospitality courses – 30 on his own course. All had managerial experience and the students came from 33 countries.

Nicholas had originally chosen to do history because it was the subject he had most enjoyed at A-level. He had no career ideas and deliberately decided to choose a non-vocational course – with the intention of taking a postgraduate conversion course later. '*I did that because I did not wish to be committed. I wanted to keep my options open and have some thinking time as far as jobs were concerned.*' Both his parents are doctors, so was there any pressure to take a vocational course? '*No. They were quite happy with my decision.*'

Reading had a particularly flexible system. Nicholas had to take three subjects for the first two terms. He chose politics as one subject and accounting as the other. (This was to prove a useful additional skill later on.) The second and third years of the course were also flexible. There was considerable scope to tailor the course according to personal interest. Nicholas chose to take modules in areas new to him such as US history and the US political system in addition to ones from his A-level areas of English and European history.

The skills Nicholas gained from his history degree ...

★ The ability to see both sides of an argument.
★ Awareness of different cultures.
★ Skill in reading around a topic from all angles and making a balanced judgement.
★ Decision making: 'Ultimately when writing an essay you have to come down on one side or the other. And you must be able to back up your view, right or wrong.'
★ Communications skills: 'very important when I am explaining figures and charts to colleagues'.
★ 'The ability to empathise and put myself in the position of someone who was going through events as they happened in different historical periods. This is very important in dealing with people and being aware of how they might react to explanations, criticism or instructions from me.'

... and from university life in general

★ Organisational skills.
★ Communication and people management skills.

In Nicholas's final year he was a member of the hall of residence student committee. Through this he gained experience in costing and organising student balls and special events such as Valentine's Day parties. The committee also acted as a link between residents and hall managers, raising issues and complaints from the students.

Nicholas's advice

'If you have no clear career ideas I would always say do a degree in a subject you already know. It's a big jump into the unknown to study something completely new for three years. You can always get your specialist knowledge on a postgraduate course as I did – and even that did not narrow my options too much. As it was a broad management course I could have chosen other types of management work or specialised in tourism.

'I was prepared to do the extra course though, which might not be everyone's choice. Both my parents did a lengthy training, so there is a tradition of study in my family.'

Career note

As Nicholas explains, it is possible to join some companies on a graduate training programme. Applicants will however be in competition with students from degree courses in hotel and catering. A postgraduate diploma course and/or a period of suitable work experience can give wider opportunities.

Philip Murphy
Patrol Sergeant, Thames Valley Police Force

A-levels: English Literature, History, Geography.
Degree: Modern History and International Relations (2:1), University of Reading.

Philip did his degree course on an Army bursary, as he fully intended to join the Military Police after university. Under this scheme he attended university as a civilian but received an annual sum of money from the Ministry of Defence. This was similar to receiving sponsorship from an employer, the only difference being that he was committed to completing officer training after graduation. The degree choice was his. The Army put no pressure on him to choose a particular subject.

He had completed a UCAS form but during his A-level year decided to apply to the Army instead. He did however keep the UCAS application live in case he was not accepted.

> 'I was in Wiltshire at the Regular Commissions Board on the day of the A-level results. I rang from there for my results. When I told the selectors that they were AAB they immediately said that if I passed the Board successfully I should defer entry to Sandhurst and apply for a bursary to do a degree course. I was accepted and spent four weeks before term started on an introductory course at Sandhurst. My sponsors throughout my time at Reading were the Royal Military Police.'

Philip thoroughly enjoyed his degree course:

> 'All the subjects were interesting. It wasn't like studying at all. The course was very flexible with a lot of choice. I had been fascinated by both the military and by history from about the age of seven. I concentrated where I could on the Second World War and post-war conflict.'

What Philip did not enjoy was the fact that as an Army bursary holder he was expected to join the university's Officer Training Corps. He had been a cadet at school and so felt that he was going over old ground. He gained permission from the Military Police to become a Special Constable with the local police force instead and did that for two years. The experience was enjoyable and he began to have seeds of doubt about military police work – but was committed.

Philip's decision was virtually made for him. During his course at Sandhurst he broke both legs while taking part in an exercise and missed so much of the course that he would have had to lose a year and start all over again. He took the plunge, asked for permission to leave and applied to join the Thames Valley Force where he had worked as a Special.

His current job as a patrol sergeant is what Philip describes as hands-on people management. When he is on duty he is in charge of eight constables – his patrol or team. He briefs them at the start of each shift, allocates duties and throughout the shift might be called on for assistance by any one of them.

There are certain incidents such as fatal accidents or suspicious deaths that he must attend. He must constantly motivate his team and encourage them when they are under pressure. He is also called on to make instant decisions. *'Sometimes in a difficult situation they will tread water until I get there. Then the buck stops with me!'* In addition Philip is responsible for appraising his constables, helping to plan their career moves and recommending them for promotion. His own next step up the ladder will probably be to work in a specialist role to gain further experience and then to become an inspector. He has already worked as a traffic officer.

Skills Philip gained from his course ...

★ Ability to assimilate a large amount of information and to evaluate it. 'I have to hold a lot of knowledge of criminal law in my head and be able to apply it to situations instantly. Frequently circumstances mean that I can't go to consult a legal reference book before making a decision.'

★ 'Two skills in particular: report writing and giving evidence. Writing reports is the bane of a police officer's life. I have to prepare a lot of papers for court. There is tricky legalistic jargon and everything must be presented in a style barristers, solicitors and judges relate to. Non-graduates do find this more difficult, I think. Giving evidence in court is in effect making a presentation – and expecting to be questioned on it. I had been doing this in seminars since I was 18. Again, I feel that graduates are less nervous than non-graduate entrants.'

★ Ability to study independently. (Police officers who wish to gain promotion have to work in their own time in order to pass examinations. The examination for promotion to sergeant is particularly detailed.)

... and from being at university

'I gained experience of a wider society – different people from all classes and creeds. I come from a small mining village in Durham. It was a very insular world. I had never met anyone from any of the ethnic minorities. I had no idea that people existed who didn't worship football! I could relate to toughies on the street. But university gave me the confidence to relate to professional people too. That is very important in my job, where some members of the public think police officers are as thick as planks!'

Philip's advice

'I would say never do a vocational course unless you are 100% certain of what you want to do. It is too easy to get sucked into going in a certain direction. The expectation of family and friends is that you will go where the subject leads you. The beauty of arts courses is that they are so general and so varied that you are able to keep most doors open.

'Another advantage is that as other people on your course are going in different directions you are not rivals. I had friends doing law who were all applying to the same employers in their final year. They were in direct competition, always looking over their shoulders and wondering whether what they said in seminars might affect their references.'

Career note

An increasing number of graduates now join the police force although it is not necessary to have a degree in order to do so. A small number join under a highly selective accelerated programme designed to take them rapidly to the rank of inspector. Others join in the normal way. Whatever their qualifications on entry, all police officers must gain experience as constables for two years before applying to take the sergeants' examination.

History of Art

Myth. History of art is a vocational course. All graduates go into picture restoration (wrong – this is a career that requires specialist practical and technical skills), into fine art valuation, antique dealing or art gallery management. Some do enter the last three careers. These are the directly vocational possibilities, as are art critic (a very small field), museum curator and inspector of historic buildings. (Most openings for this work – and there are not many – are with the national heritage organisations.)

Related occupations, those in which the degree is particularly relevant, include heritage management, picture research, librarianship and publishing.

But history of art is a rigorous academic discipline. There is no reason why graduates in the subject should not become accountants, computer programmers, barristers, marketing managers …

By studying this subject you gain almost identical skills to those gained on a general history course (see Chapter 5, page 50).

What do Graduates do? does not cover art history but HESA figures show that:

★ 100 entered the occupational category **Managers and Administrators**.
  Of these, 40 were specialist managers; 20 were managers and proprietors in service industries; 30 were managers and administrators 'not elsewhere classified'.
★ 50 entered **Professional Occupations**.
  20 went into teaching; 30 into librarianship and related professions.

- ★ 80 entered **Associate Professional and Technical Occupations**.
  50 as literary, artistic and sports associate professionals.
- ★ 90 entered **Clerical and Secretarial Occupations**.
  30 went into general clerical work; 20 as secretaries and personal assistants; 10 as receptionists.
- ★ 20 entered **Personal and Protective Service**.
  10 went into catering.
- ★ 70 entered S**ales and Related Occupations**.
  10 as sales representatives; 50 as sales assistants.

(Total number of students surveyed = 440.)

HESA figures are for students who graduated in 1999/2000.

All figures relate to graduates who went straight into employment. They do not include those doing postgraduate courses.

And these figures should be treated with caution. Compiled six months after students have graduated, they are bound to include some who are in temporary jobs to gain experience or to earn a living while making applications for 'graduate-level' jobs. If asked their whereabouts six months after graduating both Tim Youngs and Rebecca Hon, for example (see pp 78 and 29), would have given their destinations as 'Clerical', whereas both used those jobs as stepping stones to satisfying careers.

Emma Hanham
Production Secretary, BBC

A-levels: History of Art, History, Theology.
Degree: Art History and Theology (2:1), University of Bristol.

Emma's job involves work on three programmes in the Documentaries Department. Currently these include one current affairs programme and two docu-soaps.

'The work is administrative and mainly based in my office – but I do get to go out sometimes. If I'm out with the film crew once the cameras have started rolling I act as an extra pair of eyes for directors. They can't see what is going on out of camera range whereas I can make sure that the camera crew are not going to bump into anyone and that no accidents happen. I might also have to get permissions. On a filming trip at Heathrow Airport one of my duties was to run after passers-by who had been included in shots, explain this to them and obtain their permission to be filmed.

'It is an incredibly interesting job. I sort out everything connected with filming, from clearing rights to use a piece of music, to making sure that we can definitely get into places, to keeping an eye on the budget.

'Most of my days are spent on the administrative work connected with programmes. Today, for instance, my first job was to finalise the arrangements for some foreign filming. I started by briefing the camera crew and sound manager. (My manager knows all the good camera men and women and she had made sure she got the ones she wanted.) I had already organised their flights and hotels, so I now had to give them their tickets and some currency.

'Then I moved on to work for a future programme. I was organising permission to use a piece of music. That meant clearing copyright with the owner and agreeing a payment. When I wasn't on the phone I got on with typing up the transcript of some interviews that had been recorded earlier for another programme. I have to be very organised. I spend a lot of time on the phone – and on my computer.

'This job is a first step for me. To get into the BBC in any capacity is very competitive. It is a question of getting a foot in the door. Now that I am here I shall watch for an opportunity to move into research. One way is to do my own research first – do some background work and try to find a producer who would give me a trial as an inexperienced researcher.'

Emma liked all her A-level subjects equally, so chose her degree course as a means of keeping up her interest in all of them. She had vague ideas that she was *'heading toward an arty, media slot – something creative or involving writing'* and had organised her school work experience placement in an art gallery. She then, as she says, bounced cheerfully through university until her last year, when she began to think seriously about a career. It was here that she benefited from an excellent course organised by her careers advisory service. She attended a three-day course on the media, on which students working in small groups did role play exercises as imaginary journalists and also wrote an eight-minute television drama piece. Their efforts were judged by Nick Parkes (of *Wallace and Grommit* fame) and a presenter from BBC Bristol.

Emma knew now what she wanted to do and wrote to BBC Bristol asking to do some unpaid work experience. She was accepted and worked there on a wildlife project. *'I researched material in their library, did odd jobs – but, most important, saw how things were done and met producers.'*

Two years later Emma landed her permanent job. Before then she did more unpaid work, this time on a national magazine (and gained useful experience in writing pieces for their promotions department), spent several months travelling, did a secretarial course, then settled down to a jobhunt.

> 'I did several temporary jobs for an agency, events organisation at Olympia and Earls Court. The best thing I did was to enrol with the temp agency. They had me down for television work and had access to vacancies I would never have found by myself. Eventually, they found me the job here.'

Skills Emma gained on her degree course ...

★ Ability in essay writing – which easily translates into report writing.
★ 'The ability to focus my mind and to narrow down ideas.'
★ Research skills – how to sort the relevant from the irrelevant.

Emma's Advice

> 'Get a good class of degree in a subject you enjoy. This impresses employers in my career area as much as one of the apparently relevant degrees. However, when I graduated I

was a well-rounded person but not immediately employable. It is essential to gain some work-related skills, whether you do so during your time at university or afterwards as I did. I learned all my administrative skills on my secretarial course and in my various office jobs. My temp jobs also taught me how to use different computer systems. If you are aiming for a career in the media it is essential to have some relevant work experience behind you. This will nearly always have to be unpaid – so you will need to have earned or saved some money to support yourself while doing it.'

Career note

Getting into broadcasting is notoriously difficult. Few companies run formal training schemes, other than for news journalists. Some form of work experience is essential – and many successful applicants begin as Emma did by getting a foot in the door in an administrative capacity.

Lisa Kelly
Department Manager, John Lewis Department Store, Cribbs Causeway

A-levels: Social and Environmental Biology, English Language, Social and Economic History.
Degree: History of Art with History (2:1), University of Bristol.

Lisa had always enjoyed art – and if she had felt that she had any talent for the practical side would have taken it as a fourth A-level. So when it came to degree course choice it seemed natural to choose history of art – to indulge her creative side – together with history, which was her strongest subject. She also had the idea of a career using art history in mind and was thinking about work in art dealing, valuation, gallery management or museum curatorship.

To her surprise history of art was not creative. It was similar to history, which formed 25% of the course.

'I loved the style of work. I loved the opportunity to do my own research and spent hours in the library doing the sort of work that had not been possible at A-level – reading stacks of information and evaluating other people's opinions. Some of the topics I just hadn't anticipated at all, like the influence some way-out philosophers had had on French painters and how others had been influenced by Wagner's music. In the first year the two subjects were quite unrelated but from then, when I had more choice I deliberately chose options on the history side that would complement the history of art.'

Lisa's career plans received a jolt almost as soon as she started her course.

'I realised that there were limited openings in galleries unless you were rich enough to own one or had friends who collected art, and the idea of working at the bottom of the heap for years in a national gallery or museum – until I got a chance of promotion – was not appealing.'

She was finding her academic work so interesting, however – and so time consuming – that she had no time to give to thinking about alternative careers: 'Suddenly I was in my third year and beginning to panic, thinking, "What am I going to do?"'

So Lisa went to her careers service hoping to find an answer. She tried everything, she says, completed computerised questionnaires, attended a presentation on careers in the media – which appeared every bit as competitive as art history – but, other than deciding against a postgraduate course, was no further forward. She then decided to concentrate on finals.

'I really did work very hard to get my degree and I was so wrapped up in finals that I felt sure I wouldn't come over well at milk round interviews. I simply had no time to spend on preparing elaborate presentations.'

After graduating Lisa decided to take time out to travel and took a full-time job in a restaurant to finance it. She had worked as a waitress during her degree course and was fortunate in having no debts to repay. She loved the work, earned a good salary through 'incredible tips' and impressed the managers so much that she was soon promoted to supervisory level. This increased her confidence and she felt ready to leave and manage another restaurant. She enjoyed this too – and the travelling never happened.

Three years later Lisa realised that this was not what she wanted to do for the rest of her life: '*There was no intellectual stimulus. I was not using my brain and the company I was with gave me no long-term security. There was no sick pay or pension scheme.*' She went back to Bristol University's careers service. There she analysed her own skills and found that they matched those required in retailing, while the John Lewis Partnership (JLP) matched her personal requirement to work for an employer with principles that agreed with her own.

Lisa applied to the Bristol store and was invited to attend an assessment day. She prepared well by watching the JLP video in the careers information room, reading about the company and visiting some of the stores. Doing this helped in the interviews, but it was her previous experience that helped in the selection exercises.

> 'There were several during the day. In one we all in turn had to pick a card with the name of a charity on it and give our reasons to the rest of the group for recommending that JLP should make a donation to it. Mine was a particularly obscure one and I had to think on my feet fast. I was the only candidate that day to go forward to the next stage. I honestly don't think I would have been chosen if I had applied during my final year at university.'

During the second stage interviews Lisa was asked the obvious sorts of questions, such as 'What are we looking for in a manager?' and more searching ones, concentrating on her personal skills. She was also asked to take to the interview something that demonstrated a strong interest or commitment to a spare-time activity. She chose to take photographs of furniture that she had painted as a hobby.

Lisa was chosen to join JLP's management development programme at the Cribbs Causeway store near Bristol. She was placed in a department to work as a selling assistant and given a training diary with targets to complete. The aim was to experience all aspects of sales work and to reach junior management level in one year. Lisa did so in three months.

> 'I worked my socks off again, spent evenings working on my assignments and preparing presentations and set my own

targets for each month. I found my degree training was very useful in helping me to write concise reports.'

In her present job Lisa is in charge of half of Ladies' Fashions and has a team of 30 staff. Three are section managers – one responsible for lingerie, swimwear and nightwear, another for outerwear and the third for administration. The rest of the staff are sales advisers or, as JLP calls them, partners. (Lisa is a management partner.) What does she do in a typical day?

'The first thing is to check staffing levels. I need to know that I have enough assistants to cover each section and will already have planned for holidays or training courses. If people are absent through sickness or emergencies I'll have to go to the staff office and ask for help from other departments. I meet the section managers next and ask whether they have any problems, then I tackle my in-tray. I put my memos in priority order and decide an order for acting on them. I think that years of working in a small space in a library have helped me to be a very neat worker. I hate a messy desk! For the rest of the day I spend regular periods on the sales floor to check whether the team is having any difficulties, monitor customer service and make sure that I take time to chat to all my staff. In my time off the floor I could be holding training sessions, thinking out strategies to develop sales, meeting with my managing director to discuss my results, or maybe planning some evening in-store events. I have to constantly analyse sales and wastage figures (wastage means goods that are damaged or lost in transit) and think of ways to improve them. I always have some kind of project on the go, for myself on aspects of running this department or perhaps for the managing director on ways of pushing the business forward and making our store stand out. It is my job to make things happen.'

What does she like about her job?

'The sheer variety. No two days are ever the same. Managing a team of people. And – the fact that in this company I can manage in a way that I like. People are treated with dignity. There is a genuine democracy, with partners' views asked for all the time.'

The skills Lisa gained from her degree ...

★ Time management.
★ Self-discipline: 'I had six hours' lectures each week. I had to motivate myself to go to the library and work.'
★ Ability to handle paperwork and to prioritise.
★ Decision-making ability. 'I learned to do my own research and to analyse. I am sure that being a graduate helps me in the strategic planning side of my job.'

... and from work experience

★ Ability to work in a team.
★ Leadership.
★ Willingness to delegate: 'It's difficult to learn to let go and to trust your staff to do things rather than to keep tight control yourself.'

Lisa's advice

'I would love to have been born knowing that I wanted to be a vet. I wasn't. If you have no burning career ambition, resist all pressure to do a "useful" subject and do something that you want to do. You will be surprised at the number of skills you gain from doing a subject that you enjoy doing.'

Career note

Most of the major retailers run graduate training schemes. They vary in length from company to company but typically include periods working as an assistant in different selling departments, as a supervisor and in off-the-floor departments such as human resources, marketing or accounts. While training, graduates usually attend short courses with other management trainees and are often given projects to complete.

7 Modern Languages

These are subjects that sound much more vocational than they really are. We are frequently told that the British are very bad at learning languages and that people of other nationalities are at an advantage through their willingness to learn one if not more foreign languages. So surely any British student proficient in languages should find the world their oyster and employers queuing up to offer them jobs? Well, no, unfortunately. The point is that languages are skills. They are an asset but rarely a career in themselves.

The only directly related careers are teaching, interpreting and translating. Of these, interpreting (the spoken word) is the smallest. Very, very few people indeed earn a living through interpreting alone. Most combine it with translating (the written word) and even then may have to supplement their earnings by teaching.

However, modern linguists are extremely employable! They automatically possess the additional skills of being able to communicate in different languages. There are many careers in the field of business and commerce where this is an advantage – from banking to insurance, marketing to law, accountancy to purchasing, distribution to logistics management, not to mention the more obvious areas of the Civil Service (including the diplomatic service), the European Union institutions, travel, tourism and hospitality.

Then, in addition to specific linguistic skills, language students acquire a good many more skills from studying their subjects. They are first and foremost communicators. They spend large amounts of time speaking, discussing and making presentations. They can communicate well in writing. They have the general essay-writing skills of any arts graduate but they have also learned to be very precise in their use of language. Translation calls at the same time for accuracy and creative use of language. The text translated must be accurate but it must also sound as though it had been written in the new language. This requires excellent skill in manipulating the English language. Using the foreign languages requires more accuracy – and care (all those grammar rules and the verb endings that must agree). Many languages graduates use their skills in careers where accuracy and attention to detail are required, such as law, journalism and publishing. Others become computer programmers – a job that requires logical ability.

Language graduates have usually spent a period abroad. The added independence they have gained from this experience plus the understanding of other cultures makes them valuable to many employers. One or two people who feature as case studies in this book refer to the period spent in other countries as especially valuable in their personal development.

What do Graduates do? shows that most language graduates move into the same category of administrative work as other arts graduates and in roughly the same proportion. About the same number enter commercial, industrial and public sector management – approximately the same percentage as historians; more than English graduates. More enter marketing, advertising and sales than students from the other two subjects. More enter the media than do history graduates, but fewer – perhaps not surprisingly – than English graduates.

Some of the surprises?

★ Army officer
★ Business analyst
★ Corporate finance analyst
★ Fund manager
★ Trainee art dealer.

HESA statistics show that:

★ 350 entered the occupational category **Managers and Administrators**.
Of these, 150 were specialist managers; 40 were financial institutions and office managers or Civil Service executive officers; 40 were managers and proprietors in service industries; 100 were managers and administrators 'not elsewhere classified'.

★ 240 entered **Professional Occupations**.
170 went into teaching; 50 into business and finance.

★ 210 entered **Associate Professional and Technical Occupations**.
20 as computer analysts and programmers; 80 as business and finance associate professionals; 10 as social welfare associate professionals; 70 as literary, artistic and sports associate professionals.

★ 370 entered **Clerical and Secretarial Occupations**.
20 in the Civil Service and local government; 30 as numerical clerks and cashiers; 30 as filing and records clerks; 170 into general clerical work; 70 as secretaries and personal assistants; 30 as receptionists.

★ 60 entered **Personal and Protective Service**.
20 went into catering; 10 as travel attendants and into related occupations; 20 went into childcare and related occupations.

★ 100 entered **Sales and Related Occupations**.
20 as buyers, brokers and related agents; 30 as sales representatives; 40 as sales assistants.

(Total number of students surveyed = 1360.)

NB. The *What do Graduates do?* information refers to 1999 graduates. The new edition was due out very shortly after this book was written. HESA figures are for students who graduated in 1999/2000.

All figures relate to graduates who went straight into employment. They do not include those doing postgraduate courses.

And these figures should be treated with caution. Compiled six months after students have graduated, they are bound to include some who are in temporary jobs to gain experience or to earn a living while making applications for 'graduate-level' jobs. If asked their whereabouts six months after graduating both Tim Youngs and Rebecca Hon, for example (see pp 78 and 29), would have given their destinations as 'Clerical', whereas both used those jobs as stepping stones to satisfying careers.

Jeremy Silverman
Management Consultant, Accenture

A-levels: French, Spanish, Economics.
Degree: French and Spanish (2:1), University of Bristol.

Jeremy chose his degree course for pure interest. He liked the literature and language content of both subjects and wanted to study them in more depth. He was aware that a degree in modern languages leads to very few careers directly, but was also aware that linguists entered a wide range of careers – and that knowledge of languages could be an asset in many jobs. At that time he was vaguely considering banking or general business management as possibilities.

He started to think about careers seriously in his second year. None of the lecturing staff, he reasoned, would be likely careers experts so he went to make use of Bristol's careers service. There he found a lot of useful information, including self-assessment questionnaires and information on different careers. Particularly helpful was the file containing contact details of former graduates who were willing to talk about their jobs.

Business seemed a good option, so Jeremy joined AISEC, a society for students interested in business and commerce. He attended their events, helped to organise some meetings with visiting speakers and made full use of a series of workshops on topics such as time management and interview skills: '*I knew that I had a limited amount of time and that I ought to use it wisely*.' He also did a vacation placement with a large firm of accountants – which made him realise that that profession was not for him: *'I was looking for something with a lot of variety that would give me exposure to all levels of a company.'*

So what does a management consultant do?

'My firm is in the business of helping companies to increase their profits and/or make changes in order to become more competitive or to enter new markets. What I actually do varies. I never do exactly the same thing from one month to another. That is one of the aspects of the job that I enjoy. I now specialise in energy and utilities. I work for companies all over the world and help them to devise new strategies or to change the way in which they do business.

'I never work alone, always in a team. Teams are brought together for different projects – so the colleagues I work with on one project may not be the same as I worked with on the last one. Teams always have a pyramid structure with a partner in charge and, in descending order, a number of senior managers, managers, analysts and consultants. The team can also change during the project. We may start off with a large team, then as some people contribute their expertise they leave to go to another project and new people are brought in. For example, on deregulation of the electricity supply industry we were called in to help a major regional supplier. They needed to reassess their business procedures, technology systems and develop a high-level strategy. They were going to be competing in a totally new market and wanted to become the market leader. So we developed a blueprint for them. At the beginning the team had a handful of members – and three or four managers who saw the project through. At one point there were 30 or 40 people working with the client and then as the work came to an end the numbers dropped again. The project lasted about a year.

'I'm currently working with a large utility company in Texas. (Deregulation is also happening in the USA.) We are doing five or six small projects for them. My involvement is in implementing a trading and risk management IT system.

'I have worked in several countries. Sometimes, as in Spain and Switzerland, my languages have been an asset. But I have also worked in the UK, the USA, Germany and the Netherlands.'

What skills does a management consultant need?

According to Jeremy:

★ 'You must be a team player.
★ You need to be well presented on all fronts, professional and a good communicator.
★ Analytical skills.
★ The ability to take in a large amount of information.
★ Willingness to learn technology.
★ Patience.
★ You must not be work-shy. The hours are long.'

The skills Jeremy gained from his degree ...

★ Analytical ability.
★ Accuracy and attention to detail (from translation work).
★ Communication skills: 'through the chance to express yourself in a group setting. Seminars are very different from "chalk and talk".'
★ Discussion: 'listening to other people's points of view *and* holding my own – fighting for my opinion'.

... and from student life in general

★ Time management (balancing academic work with involvement in AISEC).
★ Again through AISEC – leadership and organisational ability.

Jeremy's advice

'Start to research possible careers in your second year. In fact the first year would be better. Don't leave it too late. Assess your own values first. You need to know whether your priority is to earn a lot of money, to settle down and find security, to work for a charity – or whatever. Ringing potential employers comes last!'

Career note

Management consultancies put graduates through their own training programmes. Most of the major recruiters accept students in any subject (although a few prefer IT or business studies graduates). A high level of numeracy is important and some employers prefer applicants with language skills.

Tim Youngs
Library Clerk, House of Commons

A-levels: French, German, Geography.
Degree: German and Russian (2:1), University of Bristol.
MA in Slavonic and East European Studies, University of
London.

Unlike many people, Tim did give some thought to his future
career before applying to university.

'When I chose my degree course it was a straight choice
between geography and languages. I was enjoying all my
A-level subjects. I spoke to a careers adviser and discussed
job possibilities from each degree. In the end I decided that,
since I had a strong interest in international affairs, a degree
that combined the study of two languages with the culture,
literature and history of two countries would be my best
option. Although I had no firm career in mind I was aware of
some options. The RAF, intelligence work and the Foreign
Office were all in my mind. I was also prepared for the fact
that an MA might be necessary to give me an advantage
when applying for that kind of job.

'My French was at a higher level than my German, so I
decided to continue with German and begin a new language.
I hesitated over Chinese; then chose Russian.

'I had to work hard at the Russian. Some people on the
course had A-level; others GCSE. I was in the beginners'
group, as were most people.'

Tim began to think seriously about a career in his final year. No
organisations recruiting graduates appealed to him but by now
he had decided that he was prepared to put some time into
making the right choice and into gaining some suitable
experience. He decided to move to London and take some
temporary jobs, while gaining some basic skills in office work.

What did it feel like to be one of the few not jobhunting?
*'Strange, even nerve-racking. Most other students were keen to
start earning. I was bucking the trend and felt I was perhaps
missing out on making applications.'*

Instead of joining the milk round, Tim took a series of temporary jobs – which acted as valuable stepping stones. The first, administrative work for an international charity, gave him a good grounding in office systems and taught him how to use computers. In the second, he says, he really landed on his feet (what he did in fact was to make use of opportunities that arose there): *'It was a temporary job at the European Commission office in London. I did some report writing in my own time – on relationships between the EU and eastern European countries. I showed these to people at the Commission and received encouragement.'*

Tim did his MA partly financed by a Career Development Loan, did some more work for a charity when the course ended (this time as a volunteer) and then spotted an advertisement for the position at the House of Commons. The job has a misleading title. Known as a *library clerk*, Tim is actually a highly skilled research analyst.

'I am a *Servant of the House* (that is, employed by Parliament itself, not the Civil Service). The job has lots of variety. Five of us specialise in different areas of the world. I cover Russia and Eastern Europe – but I have had to become a specialist on the Middle East too. I write four or five major research papers each year. I enjoy a certain amount of freedom in choosing the subject matter, although this is dictated to a certain extent by world events and the parliamentary timetable. I have recently written papers on Iraq, the Balkans and the Middle East Peace Process.

'I also write short briefing notes on current issues in my areas and take my turn at the enquiry desk in the Members' Library, which I find particularly interesting. We receive all kinds of enquiries – such as preparing background information for an MP who is due to make a speech that evening, or giving a spontaneous ten-minute briefing on a foreign country to help with an interview on *World at One*! Therefore I need to spend a lot of time reading and staying up to date. But I do that anyway. I read periodicals such as *The Economist* and I watch current affairs programmes in my own time.

'The most interesting aspect of the job for me is the almost total lack of routine and the large amount of autonomy I

enjoy. I also have interesting career prospects. I could apply
for a secondment to the Foreign and Commonwealth Office,
the Cabinet Office or the European Commission in Brussels.
Although I am not in the Civil Service itself I am on the same
grade as their fast-stream entrants, and postings to gain
experience in other departments' work are encouraged.'

Skills Tim gained from his degree course?

★ The ability to sift through and analyse large quantities of
  information.
★ Development of good analytical writing skills.
★ Time management.
★ Skill in prioritising a workload.
★ The ability to summarise different perspectives and present
  an impartial point of view: 'Studying literature helped in this
  respect as there are no correct answers in that subject.
  Impartiality is possibly one of the greatest assets I have
  gained from my studies.'
★ *And* the year spent abroad was of real value: 'I spent six
  months in Germany and six in Russia. It took me away from
  familiar surroundings and taught me to adapt to different
  cultural circumstances.'

Career note
There is no set route into Tim's job. Jobs are advertised as they
arise. Entry is very competitive and having a higher degree is an
advantage.

John Howden
Contract Officer, Public Sector Management

A-levels: French, Business Studies, English Literature, General
Studies.
Degree: English and French (2.2), Chester College of Higher
Education.

How did John choose his degree course?

'I was interested in drama at school and chose English and
drama at first. Chester appealed because of its smallness and
the intimacy of its campus. Also Chester is such a nice city.

However, after a term, I decided that I really still enjoyed French and should not have dropped it. The flexible arts degree system at college allowed me to change to English and French.'

He had not decided exactly what he wanted by the end of his course so he went to the Job Centre on the Wirral, where he lives, discovered that there was a temporary vacancy at the Job Centre itself and applied for it. He became an administrative officer with responsibilities for undertaking fortnightly job reviews with local job seekers, dealing with Job Seeker Allowance payments and helping people find and apply successfully for jobs in the area. He had to learn how to use the Job Centre IT systems to search out details of each client and vacancy.

The contract lasted seven months, by which time he had learned a fair amount about the local employment and job training scene, including that the Chester, Ellesmere Port and Wirral Training and Enterprise Council (CEWTEC) had the responsibility for drawing down government funding for training for employment and training in the Wirral area. The logical next move, when his Job Centre contract ran out, was to build on his increasing knowledge of local employers and he secured his current post of contract officer with CEWTEC.

'I now have a case load of around 90 employers. My job is to visit, roughly every three months or so, all young people working as Modern Apprentices with any of those employers. CEWTEC was the main local source of funding for Modern Apprenticeships and was responsible for ensuring that young people receive the quality of training that the system promises. In effect I help to make sure that the government gets value for money for its investment in training offered to young people by employers in our area. My companies range from motor vehicle repairers to social and community care providers, early years nurseries and firms offering training in office work. I also have responsibility for record keeping and maintenance of the IT system in the CEWTEC offices.'

These days public service work stretches beyond the Civil Service and local authorities. CEWTEC was a semi-government organisation responsible for ensuring that government training policies in the area were efficiently carried out. Much of John's work would once have been done by the old Department of Employment. However, the government recently abolished Training and Enterprise Councils and put some of their former responsibilities out to contract. CEWTEC staff formed a company that successfully bid to continue the delivery of Modern Apprenticeships in the Wirral area and beyond. John was especially pleased that he won the prize for thinking up the name of the new company – *Scientiam* – from the Latin for 'knowledge'. He now has the distinction of working for a company he actually named.

John has found that it is the range of people he meets which makes his work interesting. There is a downside – the absolute requirement to meet various targets that are written into the contract which Scientiam has with the government via the Learning and Skills Council. It puts pressure on him to know that his job might be threatened if the company should fail to meet those targets – a situation which is not uncommon these days in the public sector.

He is now about to make a career move and transfer to the private sector – as a logistics planner with Esso. His language skills may well come in useful here as he will be helping plan the distribution of Esso products across Europe.

Skills John acquired from his degree course ...

★ Giving presentations: 'I had to produce work and present it to tutorial groups for discussion, during which I would have to defend my arguments against people who might take a different point of view. Presentations are a constant part of what I do now. In fact I had to make one as part of the selection process that got me the job. I am convinced that the confidence I gained doing this at Chester gave me an advantage over some of the other applicants.'

★ Report writing: 'My essay work trained me to write in a clear, concise and forceful style. It is essential that I write work reports in the same way.'

★ IT: 'You take IT in higher education for granted, simply because you use it so much during your course. But confidence in dealing with IT packages is really vital when you get to work.'

★ Producing an effective CV: 'The college careers service helped me with this towards the end of my course.'

... and from college life in general

★ People skills: 'I became really confident in dealing with the range of people I met at college – fellow students, staff and customers from my term-time job as a supervisor in a grocery store. Now I have no problems in making the first move with all the people I meet at work. They include young people and their parents, employers, careers advisers and lecturers from local colleges who help with some of the Modern Apprentice education.'

John's advice

'The thing about an arts degree is that when it comes to thinking about a career you are not restricted. There is a huge range of possibilities waiting for you. So don't be afraid to go for one if that is where your strengths lie. Although some people see arts as a bit woolly, the fact is that the practical skills you gain from them make you very employable in a wide range of careers.'

Career note

Administrative work is the largest area entered by arts graduates. It is a very wide term, covering public sector organisations such as the Civil Service, local government and the National Health Service, but also many private sector companies. It is now much easier than it used to be to switch between sectors during a career.

8 Philosophy

There is only one career that this subject leads to directly – and that is teaching (or more likely lecturing in higher education, since although the subject does exist at A-level it is not taught in many schools).

Philosophy graduates still enter a varied range of careers however. (See Introduction for examples in addition to those given here.) They have the same skills as other arts graduates – with perhaps even more emphasis on logical reasoning since most will have studied logic as an integral part of the course. This leads a significant number into careers as computer programmers and analysts. They can also understand complex arguments, produce their own conclusions – once again in an area where there are no correct answers – and give the evidence necessary to support their opinions. They can solve problems, express ideas and communicate both orally and in writing.

Philosophy can lead to the following careers in particular:

★ computing
★ information management
★ information science
★ information technology
★ insurance claims assessing
★ insurance underwriting
★ law – barrister or solicitor
★ publishing – editing, proof reading.

What do Graduates do? does not cover philosophy but destination figures kept over a five-year period by one university offering this subject show philosophy graduates working in all of the above areas plus:

★ advertising
★ banking
★ management consultancy
★ marketing
★ media sales
★ the police force
★ retail management
★ the Royal Air Force
★ social work
★ stockbroking
★ teaching English as a foreign language
★ youth work
★ and in the House of Commons library.

HESA figures show that:

★ 80 entered the occupational category **Managers and Administrators**.
Of these, 30 were specialist managers; 30 were managers and administrators 'not elsewhere classified'.
★ 50 entered **Professional Occupations**.
20 went into teaching; 20 into business and finance.
★ 50 entered **Associate Professional and Technical Occupations**.
10 as computer analysts and programmers; 10 as business and financial associate professionals; 20 as literary, artistic and sports associate professionals.
★ 100 entered **Clerical and Secretarial Occupations**.
20 as numerical clerks and cashiers; 40 went into general clerical work.
★ 30 entered **Personal and Protective Service**.
20 went into catering.
★ 40 entered **Sales and Related Occupations**.
20 as sales representatives.

(Total number of students surveyed = 380.)

HESA figures are for students who graduated in 1999/2000.

All figures relate to graduates who went straight into employment. They do not include those doing postgraduate courses.

And these figures should be treated with caution. Compiled six months after students have graduated, they are bound to include some who are in temporary jobs to gain experience or to earn a living while making applications for 'graduate-level' jobs. If asked their whereabouts six months after graduating both Tim Youngs and Rebecca Hon, for example (see pp 78 and 29), would have given their destinations as 'Clerical', whereas both used those jobs as stepping stones to satisfying careers.

Chris Michael
Assistant Editor

A-levels: Classical Civilisation, English, French, General Studies.
Degree: Philosophy (2:1), University of Birmingham.

Chris was under pressure from various sources to choose law or another job-related degree course. However, he stuck to his guns and opted for philosophy. Why?

'I had some knowledge of the subject through studying French literature. It interested me and I wanted to know more – really go into depth. I had no illusions about philosophy being a vocational subject but I knew that it would help me to think and to question. I also knew that a degree is a degree and that I might be looking for a job based on my intellectual skills rather than on subject knowledge. I did have two or three ideas at that time. One was to stay in the academic world – which would mean continuing with the subject – as a university lecturer. The other was to write in some form, maybe for a publisher of academic or specialist books. It did not seem to me that publishers necessarily gave preference to students from media studies courses. I had been told that they recruited from most disciplines.'

Chris enjoyed his degree course, in particular philosophy of language – *'because language seems to underlie all thought'*. While he liked seminar discussions he liked writing essays even more. He thoroughly enjoyed researching in the library, reading books and journals, then using all the accumulated material to direct the discussion within the essay in the way he felt was most important. This made him even more convinced that he should look for a career in publishing.

In the third year: *'everyone suddenly started to think seriously about careers'*. Chris went along to some employers' presentations arranged by the careers service but found that he was not attracted by the idea of working for a large company. He asked about one or two other careers, including marketing and accountancy, but they too held little appeal. In the end he put off jobhunting until after graduation.

He then made an appointment with a careers adviser who looked at his CV, made some suggestions and gave him useful advice on what publishers would be looking for and the type of interview questions to expect. He began to read the *Guardian* every Monday (the largest source of media and creative job advertisements) and applied for any editorial assistant posts he thought he stood a chance of getting.

It took six months to find one, during which time he improved his CV through three different work experience periods, one with a magazine publisher, one with a Web and graphic designer, one on a tabloid newspaper (all unpaid and all arranged through personal contacts): *'It was a case of I knew someone who worked at X, who knew someone else who could put me in touch with someone at Y etc.'*

Then came the first job, as editorial assistant on a puzzle magazine. Editorial assistants are normally the lowest of the low, but since this publication had a small staff Chris's duties included editing and checking puzzles, originating ideas for puzzles, compiling several himself and dealing with the freelance contributions. It was good experience and he stayed 11 months. He is now in his second job, where he works on three different trade magazines. As assistant editor his work includes writing, subbing (sub-editing) and occasionally commissioning writers.

'The magazines are *Architects' Datafile*, *Housebuilder & Developer Datafile* and *Civic & Public Building Specifier*. The editor draws up a feature list for each magazine for the whole year, so I know in advance what will be required. We normally cover three main topics in each issue. Some articles come in unsolicited in the form of press releases from manufacturers and I can choose some of these to use. They generally need subbing. For example, a door manufacturer might send in a press release of 200 words. I only need 60, so I have to cut it down to the essentials yet still keep it readable. I write a number of the longer pieces myself, using releases again or researching in more depth by contacting people for information. Sometimes I need to commission outside writers. Their work will also need subbing – including checking spelling and grammar.

'All the journals are printed in the same week, so work peaks then. I have to be organised! I know, though, that I will need four or five articles for each one so as information comes in I note it and assign it to relevant magazines. I never know until the day before printing exactly how many pages I have because the magazines depend on advertising. If the sales team suddenly get more ads in I may lose some pages. Then I have to sub all over again!'

Chris sees this job as a second stepping stone. He is now keen to move into newspapers: '*I want to stay on the editorial side but feel the subject matter and shorter deadlines will be more interesting.*' He approached the editor of his local newspaper to find out more about the way the paper works and to let the editor know what skills he could offer. Chris maintains contact with the editor, who has promised to let him know if a position becomes available.

'An advantage of working for the local newspaper is that I will be sent on a three-month editorial training course. With this qualification under my belt I should be well equipped for a career in publishing or journalism.'

Skills Chris acquired on his degree course ...

★ Deciding what is important and what is irrelevant.
★ Learning to carry out research.

★ Ability to organise a workload.
★ 'Knowing how to get to the root of a matter.'

Advice from Chris

'If you want to get into publishing you will need some work experience. No one has ever been concerned about the subject of my degree. They *have* all asked what experience I had and for evidence of commitment. I was lucky. I was one of the last students to get a grant. That meant that I did not graduate with large debts. You may have to pay tuition fees and pay back a large loan. You may not be able to afford the luxury of doing unpaid work experience when you leave university, so do it while you are there. Make use of some of the vacations – or get involved with the university newspaper during term time.'

Career note

For publishing (as opposed to journalism) it is not essential to obtain further qualifications. Most employers send their new staff on short courses held at specialist training centres. Newspaper editors will almost certainly expect their trainee journalists to work for qualifications awarded by the National Council for the Training of Journalists.

Mike Eifflaender
Pension Administrator, Hogg Robinson

A-levels: Biology, General Studies, Chemistry, English Literature.
Degree: Philosophy (2.1), University of Sheffield.

Mike had no idea about a career when he decided to apply for philosophy at Sheffield. In fact he was not even sure he wanted to study philosophy until towards the end of the first term. He was better at science at school but wanted a course that offered more independence than science, which his A-levels might have suggested. He knew that arts course teaching timetables were much more relaxed and wanted the freedom to organise his work his own way. He applied for a combined arts course at Sheffield intending to major in English literature as it was his preferred A-level subject. However, he found the philosophy part of the combination more to his taste and finished his course majoring in that.

Mike enjoyed his time at university – the reading and informal discussions with friends in the pub and the tutorial groups on the course. He was right about the freedom. In common with most arts courses there were only a few hours' formal lecturing timetabled during a typical week. Providing he met course work deadlines he could plan his life and work almost as he pleased, setting his own priorities across social life and academic work. Social life included the debating society, which he found *'particularly helpful for increasing my confidence when addressing groups of people, as I now have to do in face-to-face client meetings at work'*.

It was not until he had completed his course and left university that he began to think about the future. He had a view about the lifestyle he wished to lead – periods of employment to finance occasional extended breaks for travel. Driven by the need for income more than by the idea of career planning, he discovered that a local insurance company happened to have some one-year contracts on offer. He applied, and found himself doing clerical work in its pensions department.

All went well. He mastered the work to the extent that he could take on responsibility, deal with the day-to-day tasks and develop his interpersonal skills talking to clients on the phone and making his own decisions about how to deal with their queries. He saved his salary, left at the end of the year and indulged his taste for travelling.

On his return, Mike's experience from his first job made it relatively easy for him to find another one in the insurance and pension fields. He joined a smaller local insurance company, building on his experience by taking on more responsibility on the IT side. The lure of living in London then took hold so, after another break, he moved to his current employers – in the City.

'I work in a team of three attending to the demands of employees from over 30 companies that use Hogg Robinson to administer their staff pension schemes. Each company pays us every month a sum representing the total contributions for all the members of its scheme. I update each member's account with the month's contribution details. Following that, I ensure that the money is invested in the correct fund specified in the member's pension scheme and record the increase in value of his or her holding as it is confirmed by the fund administrators.

'I deal with hundreds of pension fund members, any one of whom might have a query on the progress and administration of his or her pension. This means that I have had to master a large and complex database. My experience on that side means that my next move in the company could be towards database management so again I have added something significant to my CV.'

The skills Mike finds essential include

★ The ability to work with a small team: 'which is almost self-managed as the supervisor's post has been vacant for some time'.
★ The confidence to talk, usually by phone, to a wide range of individual clients and contacts in the companies with which clients' contributions are invested.
★ IT skills: 'Most students take their IT skills for granted as IT is part of the furniture at university, but confidence in using computers is a big plus on a CV.'
★ Strategic thinking : 'the ability to see and aim for the long-term objectives through the mass of immediate detail – something that philosophy helped to develop.'

The skills Mike gained from his degree ...

★ Ability to prioritise and meet deadlines: 'essential for survival in the more pressurised environment of a busy office when tasks are coming at you thick and fast during a busy day'.
★ Report writing: 'Writing a philosophy essay and a report on a work-related problem might not seem the same, but I have found that both have to be written with the same clarity, focusing on the significant issues and coming to conclusions or recommendations for which a logical case has been made.'

Mike's Advice

'I am not sure, from a careers point of view, that the actual subject matters too much when you are thinking about an arts degree, so go for whatever subject interests you academically. You will probably find that most arts courses provide the opportunity to develop the same sort of skills that I have.

'The other issue is to decide on the broader issue of the sort of lifestyle you want for yourself after university. There are things I want to do with my life, such as travel, which are not work related except that I need money to pay for them. I have found that every time I take a break for travel the insurance industry seems to have vacancies to offer when I need to start work again. Not only that, but each new job is broadening my experience, adding to my CV and making me marketable in other directions. For example, I could see my next job specialising in IT management if it is not in the insurance field.'

Career note

Some insurance companies run graduate training programmes, of up to two years in length, on which new entrants spend periods in several different departments, learning about all aspects of the insurance business and about the work of other departments such as marketing, sales or e-commerce. Others recruit directly into specific jobs such as underwriting or claims assessing. Trainees are expected to study for the professional examinations of the Chartered Insurance Institute, usually through evening classes or distance learning.

People who wish to become pensions managers may join insurance companies or specialist pension consultancy firms. They would normally work for the qualifications awarded by the Institute of the Pensions Management Institute.

Careers advice and jobhunting 9

According to a survey conducted by higher education careers services, of students who graduated in 2001, 7% had started their search for employment before they began their final year; 44% had done so half-way through the year and 18% were leaving it until after graduation. In addition, 18% were going on to postgraduate study and 11% were intending to wait until they returned from travelling.

If the 44% and 18% had not begun the process until their final year they would have had to combine fitting in research into careers with work for final exams, dissertations etc. *But* they may have been putting time into research earlier on and simply had the application process to go through as finalists.

Before you can apply for a job you have to know what you want to do – not a decision that is often – or easily – made overnight. It actually takes quite a long time for most people, but help is available as long as you do not leave everything until the last minute. Your university or college will have a careers advisory service staffed by professional advisers who can help you to come to a decision. They know a great deal about different careers – and employers – and know what skills and subjects are required in different jobs. Note the phrase 'help you to come to a decision'? Students are often disappointed to find that they are not given an appointment for a magic half-hour with a careers adviser and come out at the end of that time knowing exactly what they want to do.

It takes longer than that – and involves students doing quite a lot of work. Yes, that's right. More work. The logical steps in choosing a career are:

★ self-analysis – being aware of your skills, strengths, weaknesses, values and preferences;
★ occupational awareness – knowing what is involved in different jobs;
★ making choices;
★ applying.

Careers service staff can help you through all of the above stages. Universities and colleges organise their careers services differently, but at many advisers see students from a group of departments – which means that they can become specialists in certain subjects. (So it may take some time to get an appointment with 'your' adviser.) Some advisers work closely with academic departments and give careers presentations in course time. Others have a policy under which any adviser sees any student. Some offer initial appointments of 40 minutes to an hour. Others prefer short initial advisory appointments of, say, 15 minutes, followed by further, in-depth appointments once students have done some research. You may well find that your service expects you to work your way through some questionnaires before you make an appointment.

Your careers advisory service therefore does much more than help you to find a job when you graduate. It can help you to:

★ identify any skills you need to acquire;
★ identify any experience you require;
★ organise suitable vacation experience;
★ evaluate skills gained from any part-time employment you have done;
★ work out your personal values (For instance, is it important to you to work in a profit-making environment? In a team? To achieve prestige and recognition?).

When, then, should you make contact with your careers advisory service? As early as possible! You are highly unlikely to end Freshers' Week thinking, 'OK, now I'll make that careers appointment', but the sooner you do so the more help they can give you in arranging work experience, work placements and improving the list of skills on your CV.

Jeff Goodman is the Director of the Careers Advisory Service at Bristol University. He says,

> 'At Bristol students receive a letter from the careers service outlining the service as soon as they enrol at the university. They can then sign up to be put on our weekly e-mail list. That way we can send them details of information sessions, skills workshops, employer presentations – even if they are not ready for a one-to-one meeting with a careers adviser at this stage.

> 'More and more we are being invited by staff in different subject departments to introduce ourselves to their students and explain what we can do for them. When I am talking to a particularly early group I make a joke, saying that I am like the undertaker. They will have to leave this world (of university) at some point and will need my service – but I do realise that most will wait until it becomes a real issue for them!'

One of the workshops organised at Bristol is a three-day course on working in the media, which art history graduate Emma Hanham refers to in her case study (page 64).

Your careers advisory service's resources

Most services make use of the following aids to self-analysis and career choice:

★ *Prospects Planner* – a computerised self-assessment and career matching program. You can use it at your own convenience and need not complete it in one session if you save the data. At some institutions *Prospects Planner* is networked and available for use in other places on the campus, such as the library or departmental reading rooms.
★ Pen and paper questionnaires to help you analyse your skills.
★ Various types of personality tests – for self-assessment purposes, rather than the type used at employers' selection centres.

★ Aptitude tests to measure your abilities in verbal, diagrammatic and numerical reasoning. These can be very useful for arts graduates. If you find that your numeracy is weak there is time to take remedial action before taking an employer's test.

On the information side will be:

★ a selection of files covering different occupational areas;
★ the AGCAS careers booklet series;
★ folders related to your own subject, containing career ideas and details of previous students' destinations;
★ employer files;
★ professional journals and newspapers;
★ files and prospectuses on postgraduate study;
★ information on overseas work and study;
★ reference books;
★ employer directories such as *Prospects Directory* and *Graduate Career Directory*;
★ a set of *Guides to Careers in* ... These cover areas such as finance, marketing, law – and are given away as free copies.

You will also have the chance to attend workshops on such important skills as:

★ writing a CV;
★ completing application forms;
★ what to expect from an assessment centre;
★ interview preparation and practice.

Many careers services run the workshops several times each year so that you can book in at a time convenient to you. After attending the presentation or workshop it is likely that you will be invited to draft your own CV and ask a careers adviser to comment on it and suggest any improvements. Many make use of short appointments or 'drop-in' sessions, with no appointments required, for students to do this.

Finally, when it comes to the stage of making applications for employment your careers adviser can put you in touch with employers and can give you application forms. Employers send supplies of forms, recruitment brochures and sometimes videos to careers services. Some even visit universities and colleges in person to interview students. They usually do so late in the autumn term and during the spring. A typical pattern under the milk round – mentioned in Chapter 2 – is that a recruitment manager from an organisation gives an afternoon or evening presentation, outlining the company's work, the type of careers offered and the sort of graduate they are looking for. This is followed the next day by individual first interviews with interested students. Those who are considered suitable are invited to a second interview or more often to an assessment centre in the late spring or during the Easter vacation. This still happens but less frequently than in the past. Some major recruiters still visit every university and some large colleges. But this procedure is expensive and time consuming. Others target preferred universities and the majority attend graduate recruitment fairs that are held two or three times a year and are becoming much more popular.

Sample questions from self-assessment work sheets

Personal qualities

Do you like taking risks?
Being prepared to diverge
   from the accepted line
Taking chances if necessary
Taking chances whenever
   possible
Being ready to take gambles

Examples of jobs
Broker (insurance, commodity, stock, money), merchant banker, retail buyer, entrepreneur

Are you flexible?

Readily applying yourself to new tasks

Able to adjust to new situations

Turning easily from one subject to another

Able to cope

Management services officer, administrator, secretary, auditor, journalist, social worker, management consultant

Are you resilient?

Remaining calm under pressure

Staying relaxed

Not worrying too much when things go wrong

Able to be detached – not too involved

Barrister, diplomat, teacher police officer, advertising agency account executive, production manager, social worker

Abilities

Word fluency

Ability to give accurate expression to one's meaning through speech and writing

Barrister, journalist, salesperson, civil servant, commercial manager, teacher

Perception, people

Ability to pick up people's feelings, gestures, tones of voice etc

Counsellor, teacher, salesperson, careers adviser, market researcher, social worker, industrial relations officer

Perceptions, things

Ability to notice things around you

Police officer, buyer, valuer, advertising account executive, management services officer

> **And when analysing job information ...**
>
> **What kind of social environment would you be in?**
> Who would be your colleagues?
> Other graduates?
> A wide range of people of different ages and social
> backgrounds?
>
> **How might you fit in with the job culture?**
> Are your values and philosophy compatible?
> Can you share the aims of the employing organisation?

Advice from careers advisers

Claire Rees is the Director of York University's Careers
Advisory Service. She finds that very few arts students have
made any firm career decisions before arriving at university.
Most are unaware of two facts: that there is a wide range of
options and that it can take a while to work out which ones
are suitable.

'It is tempting to want to rush in and try to identify the ideal
job. There is much more involved than that. Many students
arrive hoping that after one appointment with a careers adviser
they will be told what to do for the rest of their lives. It doesn't
work like that – and they find that they have some thinking to
do! Some find this quite challenging.'

What is Claire's advice to arts students?

'To begin by identifying their skills and values. Students often
need some encouragement to work out what skills they have
already gained – and which ones they could acquire. I might ask
them what extra-curricular activities they enjoy and why.
What have they gained from taking part in them?

'Then look at personal values. Again students can use everyday
activities in identifying these. Even mundane activities can
provide insights into yourself and the environment you are

suited to work in. If someone hated a shelf-filling job in a supermarket was this simply because the job was tedious? Or because they disliked the retail environment?

'It is important to make contact with the careers service as early as possible during the course. No later than the beginning of the second year for preference, although the end of the first year would be better. There is still time then to make use of at least one summer vacation to get some relevant work or work experience.

'Last – make full use of university life. Take part in as wide a range of activities as you can. There are plenty of opportunities. Find out what you really enjoy and are good at.'

The York service makes full use of aids to career planning such as *Prospects Planner*, plus its own self-awareness exercises, and like many careers advisory services offers students both in-depth interviews with a careers adviser that can be spent in identifying further needs and planning a course of action and the opportunity to check out quick queries through 15-minute meetings with the duty careers adviser.

Jeff Goodman says,

'Both arts *and* science graduates have access to a wide range of options. Employers increasingly look for personal skills – one of the most important being *commercial awareness*. A key element in obtaining this is work experience. If the experience is relevant that is fine but even it is not apparently so at first it may still give a considerable number of skills. For instance, I was discussing with a student yesterday the relevant merits of a summer spent on a placement with a firm of management consultants as opposed to one spent chasing a balloon round Europe. He had chosen to do the latter – and was now wondering whether consultancies would penalise him for not having any appropriate work experience on his application form. In fact, employers will value highly the skills he acquired that summer. The balloon crew were taking part in a competition. He had been responsible for staying in contact with them, predicting where they would come down each day, arranging their accommodation, and being there to meet them when they landed at each stopover point. He had had to be reliable – if he was not where he was expected the crew would have been in difficulties; he had learned to work alone for a large part of each day (developing independence and initiative); had had to make decisions; and had improved his knowledge of several languages.'

10 Books and booklets

Books and booklets

The AGCAS Careers Information series of booklets. Sample titles include:

Administration and Public Sector Management
Broadcasting, Film and Video, Theatre
City Institutions and Financial Markets
Heritage Management and Museum Work
Retail Selling, Buying and Wholesaling
Using Languages

Boosting Your Career Prospects, Trotman

Creating Winning CVs and Applications, Trotman

Developing Your Employment Skills, Trotman

Exploring Career Opportunities, Trotman

Graduate Career Directory, Hobsons (annual publication giving details of employers and their vacancies, also contains careers information in the form of job descriptions).

Graduate Salaries and Vacancies, Association of Graduate Recruiters (AGR).

How to Choose your Postgraduate Course, Trotman

How to Succeed at Assessment Centres, Trotman

Occupations, DFES (a regularly updated reference book, for information on different careers).

Promoting Yourself at Interview, Trotman

Prospects Directory, AGCAS (annual publication containing details of employers and their vacancies, see also website).

Q & A Degree Subject Guide: Studying English, Trotman/UCAS.

Skills for Graduates in the 21st Century, Association of Graduate Recruiters (AGR). Can be consulted on their website.

What do Graduates do?, published by UCAS and available from UCAS Distribution, PO Box 130, Cheltenham, Gloucestershire GL53 3ZF. Can also be found on the *Prospects* website.

Working In English
Working In History
Working In Languages – all three in a series published by the Department for Education and Skills (DFES).

Websites

Association of Graduate Recruiters, www.agr.org.uk

Careers-portal – online careers advice at www.careers-portal.co.uk

Prospects Web, a higher education careers website, www.prospects.ac.uk/student/cidd

University of London Careers Advisory Service, www.careers.lon.ac.uk – for *How to analyse and present your skills for work*

Addresses

The Historical Association, www.history.org

The Institute of Linguists, www.iol.org.uk

Careers-Portal
the Online Careers Service

Careers-Portal
has the most comprehensive information on
careers and higher education
on the web.

www.Careers-Portal.co.uk

- Facts and figures on all kinds of careers
- HE: Uncovered
- Over 2000 links to universities, job & careers sites
- Art & Design – the guide to winning the HE place you want
- And lots more...

So come online and realise
your potential!